BESTACTIVITYBOOKS.COM

Illustration Graphique Extra: www.freepik.com
Merci à Alekksall, Starline, Pch.vector, Rawpixel.com,
Vectorpocket, Dgim-studio, Upklyak, Macrovector,
Stockgiu, Pikisuperstar & Freepik.com Designers

Découvrez des Jeux Gratuits en Ligne

Disponible Ici :

BestActivityBooks.com/FREEGAMES

5 ASTUCES POUR DÉMARRER !

1) COMMENT RÉSOUDRE LES MOTS MÊLÉS

Les puzzles sont dans un format classique :

- Les mots sont cachés sans espaces, tirets, ...
- Orientation : Les mots peuvent être écrits en avant, en arrière, vers le haut, vers le bas ou en diagonale (ils peuvent être inversés).
- Les mots peuvent se chevaucher ou se croiser.

2) UN APPRENTISSAGE ACTIF

Un espace est prévu à côté de chaque mots pour noter la traduction. Pour favoriser un apprentissage actif un **DICTIONNAIRE** à la fin de cette édition vous permettra de vérifier et étendre vos connaissances. Cherchez et notez les traductions, trouvez-les dans le Puzzle et ajoutez-les à votre vocabulaire !

3) MARQUEZ LES MOTS

Vous pouvez inventer votre propre système de marquage. Peut-être en utilisez-vous déjà un ? Sinon, vous pourriez, par exemple, marquer les mots qui ont été difficiles à trouver d'une croix, ceux que vous avez aimés d'une étoile, les mots nouveaux d'un triangle, les mots rares d'un diamant, etc...

4) STRUCTUREZ VOTRE APPRENTISSAGE

Cette édition vous offre un **CARNET DE NOTES** très pratique à la fin du livre. En vacances ou en voyage ou à la maison, vous pouvez facilement organiser vos nouvelles connaissances sans avoir besoin d'un second bloc-notes !

5) VOUS AVEZ FINI TOUTES LES GRILLES ?

Allez à la section bonus **CHALLENGE FINAL** pour trouver un jeu gratuit à la fin de cette édition !

Simple et Rapide ! Découvrez notre collection de livres d'activités pour votre prochain moment de détente et **d'apprentissage**, à juste un clic de distance !

Trouvez votre prochain défi sur :

BestActivityBooks.com/MonProchainLivre

À vos marques, prêts... Partez !

Saviez-vous qu'il existe environ 7 000 langues différentes dans le monde ? Les mots sont précieux.

Nous aimons les langues et avons travaillé dur pour créer les livres de la plus haute qualité pour vous. Nos ingrédients ?

Une sélection des thématiques d'apprentissage adaptée, trois belles parts de divertissement, puis nous ajoutons une cuillère de mots difficiles et une pincée de mots rares. Nous les servons avec soin et un maximum de plaisir pour vous permettre de résoudre les meilleurs jeux de mots mêlés qui soient et d'apprendre en vous amusant !

Votre avis est essentiel. Vous pouvez participer activement au succès de ce livre en nous laissant un commentaire. Nous aimerions vraiment savoir ce que vous avez préféré dans cette édition !

Voici un lien rapide qui vous mènera à la page d'évaluation de vos commandes :

BestBooksActivity.com/Avis50

Merci pour votre aide et amusez-vous bien !

De la part de toute l'équipe

1 - Été

```
K  Q  P  V  X  B  G  S  M  Q  X  T  L  C
H  P  G  A  U  E  U  Q  Y  F  C  E  E  A
Y  U  S  C  G  A  R  D  E  N  U  A  A  R
H  E  N  A  K  C  C  X  N  B  R  G  B  A
H  O  A  T  B  H  R  E  J  V  S  H  H  I
I  G  G  I  Q  T  G  E  Ò  Z  E  L  R  D
C  C  E  O  D  E  L  N  C  L  A  A  A  E
F  C  A  N  I  A  C  A  G  D  C  C  I  A
K  D  M  Q  X  G  Q  A  O  J  H  H  C  N
B  I  A  S  T  A  R  S  M  I  A  S  H  B
R  O  N  E  D  S  E  X  Y  P  D  N  E  O
R  I  N  A  A  G  E  U  I  U  A  H  A  J
X  S  A  N  D  A  L  S  T  F  N  D  N  O
V  Z  N  E  J  X  A  W  L  X  S  I  H  Y
```

CARAIDEAN
CAMPADH
STARS
TEAGHLACH
GARDEN
NA GEAMANNAN
JOY
LEABHRAICHEAN
CUR-SEACHADAN

SEA
CEÒL
BIA
BEACH
LAOIDH
SANDALS
VACATION
TEAGASG

2 - Adjectifs #2

```
C U M H A C H D X C J E D A
F I A D H A I C H R L L E B
P R O U D S Y I A U P E S H
F S E Q P E T S I T M G C I
J L T A Y B I A N H T A R T
Z À Ù R G P O L M A D N I H
U I F Ì O R K T E C R T P A
D N B R X N A Y I H À J T N
H T M O Z C G C L A M S I P
Z E Z O W S W M H I A L V M
G A T H O I R T L L V E E C
I N N T I N N E A C H E N I
N À D A R R A U U Q T P J E
J W B N O U H Z V J I Y N B
```

FÌOR
AINMEIL
CRUTHACHAIL
DESCRIPTIVE
GA THOIRT
DRÀMA
ELEGANT
PROUD
STRONG
INNTINNEACH

NÀDARRA
ÙR
A BHITH A
CUMHACHD
EILE.
FREAGRACH
SLÀINTE
SALTY
FIADHAICH
SLEEPY

3 - Formes

```
E N A P O P O L Y G O N H S
P L V R X O V R H G O W Y I
Y C L T C E A R C A L L P O
R U L I N E L C B A Q G E L
A R T K P X A J O Y U R R A
M V R R R S P N R N A D B N
I E I C O F E F N W E S O D
D X A G I W P R I S M C L A
D S N H S N O P P Q S O A I
T L T V E I O M A L L A N R
A X A T A O B H U Y O V L N
A O N D N L H A J X Q N U G
L N D F F P P R C U B E A A
R E J O P A B C Z M O R T V
```

ARC   SIOLANDAIR
IOMALLAN   ELLIPSE
CEANN   HYPERBOLA
CEARCALL   LINE
OISEAN   OVAL
CURVE   POLYGON
CONE   PRISM
TAOBH   PYRAMID
CUBE   TRIANTAN

4 - Salle de Bains

```
F E Q M J L O D S V F Y U B
V L J B L Y Q I N Z A M Y A
S R Q A H S X T Q V U N Y T
M I P T K W D O B A C Y M A
S O A H S T N W U V E D Y R
C T L B R A T E Q K T K M A
I C P A A S S L A O I D H I
S I H E D N A M H À I N F D
S P F V R H N K H H H C I H
O P A F K F F M M H L T E E
R B U G O X U I S G E R D A
S P O N G E S M Ù I D H Y N
S H A M P O O L E O B Q X V
T A I G H B E A G A H G I S
```

BATH
BATARAIDHEAN
SCISSORS
A-MHÀIN
UISGE
SPONGE
LAOIDH
MOLADH

PERFUME
FAUCET
SIABANN
TOWEL
SHAMPOO
BRAT
TAIGH BEAG
SMÙID

5 - Adjectifs #1

```
A D H A R T A C H C D S S F
C Y E O F A V Y Y U C E A S
H W A X I Y A U K D F G E T
U Z V E L E Z H T R Q V O P
I B Y M K O J F M O G C Ò G
D M C M Z Y A R O M A T I C
G N Ì O M H A C H A P J H F
G S H F Ò O B Y F C O V O E
G F R G R H L N C H Z S N U
T U U U M J L A O I D H E M
Z N M B L F H T D K H H S A
X V Z A N U M J Y H K S T I
G D P U T H I N M B M P C L
E L K T K H P E R F E C T I
```

GU MATH	CUDROMACH
GNÌOMHACH	ÒG
ADHARTACH	LAOIDH
AROMATIC	HEAVY
MOLADH	THIN
MÒR	PERFECT
CHUID	DEEP
HONEST	FEUMAIL

6 - Instruments de Musique

```
S M O M A N D O L I N M G V
P Q B P I A N O V I O L I N
S M O O A S P V S A X K D Z
Z A E K F M F U C B E M A N
D R C U L H O I L A Z V T Q
A I S S B B C X A S V G A R
U M D I A H V F R S W J M T
R B G V N F G Q I O D G B R
F A N I J B O F N O R A A U
A L B A O B N N E N U A I M
R W Ù I Y T G H T J M K R P
A S K R D G À Z H E H O I E
I W T S O C T R O M P A N T
M C L À R S A C H C E L L O
```

BANJO
BASSOON
CLARINET
FLÙR
GONG
GIOTÀR
CLÀRSACH
OBOE
MANDOLIN
MARIMBA

FARAIM
PIANO
SACSAFON
DRUM
TAMBAIRIN
TROMPAN
TRUMPET
VIOLIN
CELLO

7 - Échecs

```
C D U B H P D M M T B J P U
Q H F X D W G Ù W X M G L C
G E A M A T R N B N H D A N
D C N M N L R K G H J H Y R
I X T M P R I N G E A L E O
A P L V U I H D A S C L R I
G A X I S Ì O N I E P S A N
O S A W T O W N W S O O A N
N S W P M B F A R P A I S L
A I T Q P A E E C N A C C E
L V P I S I D T F U H Q U A
P E H I X R I E X D A V O C
P M R V J T D X A E O I I H
K A A A B H A N R I G H R D
```

GEAL

CHAMPION

DÙBHALAN

DIAGONAL

GEAMA

PLAYER

DUBH

PASSIVE

A ' BHANRIGH

RING

ÌOBAIRT

RO-INNLEACHD

UAIR

FARPAIS

8 - Herboristerie

```
P A R S L E Y L I D U V F M
A R O M A T I C C W A K E M
F G D H K T R O À D I N A E
L A O I D H O N I V N Q R A
A R F I W P X R L I E G C C
V D E A J B C S E N S R I A
O E N F T A R R A G O N U N
R N N Z S S V P C R A Z I D
S S E O C I S L H E M N L U
T Y L D F L C V D D V I O B
S A F F R O N U U I G H N H
F L Ù R O V V P V E A W S T
C U L I N A R Y T N I J U Z
R O S E M A R Y N T H Y M E
```

AROMATIC	MEACAN-DUBH
BASIL	MINT
FEAR-CIUIL	OREGANO
CULINARY	PARSLEY
TARRAGON	CÀILEACHD
FENNEL	ROSEMARY
FLÙR	SAFFRON
INGREDIENT	FLAVOR
GARDEN	THYME
LAOIDH	UAINE

9 - Véhicules

```
R  A  P  F  S  C  O  O  T  E  R  N  Z  S
H  E  I  L  E  A  C  O  P  T  A  I  R  U
V  R  D  C  H  R  I  E  X  G  A  O  Z  B
B  Q  Y  O  T  A  C  S  A  I  D  H  A  M
À  T  G  Z  I  V  C  R  H  M  H  T  L  A
T  I  R  E  S  A  F  S  O  T  B  U  C  R
A  D  A  È  R  N  S  K  S  C  R  P  A  I
R  O  T  H  A  I  R  S  H  D  A  Z  B  N
F  E  R  R  Y  N  C  U  U  N  N  I  H  E
J  R  A  F  T  L  W  B  T  B  N  M  D  F
Z  C  C  C  X  S  J  W  T  U  J  A  W  I
X  T  T  P  À  M  G  A  L  S  F  I  Z  U
S  D  A  M  T  R  F  Y  E  V  Z  D  I  B
L  À  R  A  I  D  H  C  P  U  S  I  N  J
```

ADHBRANN	SHUTTLE
BÀTA	TIRES
BUS	RAFT
LÀRAIDH	SCOOTER
CARAVAN	SUBMARINE
FERRY	TACSAIDH
ROCAID	TRACTAR
HEILEACOPTAIR	TRÈAN
SUBWAY	ROTHAIR
CO	CÀR

10 - Camping

```
T  R  D  H  A  I  R  A  M  H  A  P  A  F
E  W  X  À  I  J  A  B  X  A  P  S  L  O
N  W  D  G  N  K  Y  L  D  M  S  O  A  R
T  P  L  C  M  A  Y  I  N  M  L  R  O  E
M  N  H  F  E  B  C  F  Z  O  A  Ò  I  S
O  P  Q  D  A  J  G  H  X  C  K  P  D  T
I  J  C  Q  C  C  V  D  K  E  R  H  D
R  M  E  Q  H  A  B  U  R  N  U  I  G  H
E  A  S  K  A  T  S  X  I  A  M  O  O  N
Z  A  D  K  D  B  E  D  I  T  Z  M  X  R
K  R  F  D  H  D  A  I  F  U  M  R  M  R
C  A  N  O  E  S  L  B  N  R  P  A  C  S
C  A  B  I  N  I  G  A  H  E  O  D  R  B
Q  O  M  I  G  B  X  J  R  F  K  H  S  S
```

AINMEACHADH	TEINE
DÀNACHD	FOREST
IOMRADH	HAMMOCK
CABIN	DH'
CANOE	LAKE
AIR A ' MHAPA	LAOIDH
AD	MOON
SEALG	MOIRE
RÒP	NATUR
URNUIGH	TENT

11 - Conservation

```
X S H B I S M T S N O D V P
G L X F M B T R F À T R Q E
L À L E O D B U W D M L U S
T I M C N G Z A H A X C O T
S N K O A W H I À R Q I E I
O T H S V C H L R R G E L C
R E C Y C L E L A A E A H I
G U Q S K G N E I M V K M D
A A E T G B M A N T Ì R E E
N I Y E E P Q D N U I S G E
I N S M L N C H E K B Q U J
C E S E A S M H A C H Q K W
V N G F A R O H N P O W H C
À R A I N N E A C H D W Z O
```

TÌRE
SEASMHACH
UISGE
ÀRAINNEACHD
ECOSYSTEM
FOGHLAM
ÀRAINNEAN

NÀDARRA
ORGANIC
PESTICIDE
TRUAILLEADH
RECYCLE
SLÀINTE
UAINE

12 - Écologie

```
T  M  K  B  O  A  B  Q  H  O  X  G  X  A
E  Ì  R  V  L  L  J  L  D  A  S  G  J  I
Y  C  R  U  I  N  N  E  Q  E  T  T  K  N
T  J  P  E  E  J  G  T  À  O  T  S  W  M
N  À  D  A  R  R  A  M  R  W  X  E  R  H
F  J  U  A  D  D  L  E  A  S  N  A  S  I
P  A  K  G  I  R  A  J  I  R  M  S  L  D
A  B  C  C  G  O  O  T  N  N  A  M  U  H
S  E  I  D  F  U  I  X  N  A  R  H  S  E
A  Ò  K  G  C  G  D  O  E  T  S  A  A  A
D  R  K  P  A  H  H  I  A  U  H  C  N  N
B  A  R  A  N  T  A  S  N  R  H  H  X  J
Q  E  V  X  B  G  O  I  R  E  A  S  A  N
F  L  Ò  R  A  I  D  H  K  C  A  N  D  J
```

TÌRE
DLEASNAS
SEASMHACH
AINMHIDHEAN
FLÒRAIDH
CRUINNE
ÀRAINNEAN
MARSH
MARA

NATUR
NÀDARRA
LUSAN
GOIREASAN
DROUGHT
BEÒ
BARANTAS
LAOIDH

13 - Astronomie

```
R A S T R O N O M E R C N W
S È Z S M P P L A N E T E N
R T I F R N R F O B M P B U
O X E D I F Ì N B T E A U Y
C K X P I X O U S M T N L L
A H U W H D M V E M E A A E
I X H W M E H H R E O L U Q
D Q O N Q U N E V S R A G U
U R N U I G H S A V K N A I
C R Ì O N A D H T C T Y L N
M O O N C O S M O S H F A O
J E G E A S T E R O I D X X
A N T A L A M H Y L E C Y G
S C O N S T E L L A T I O N
```

ASTEROID
PRÌOMH
ASTRONOMER
SKY
CONSTELLATION
COSMOS
CRÌONADH
EQUINOX
ROCAID
GALAXY

MOON
METEOR
NEBULA
OBSERVATORY
PLANET
RÈIDIDHEACHD
PANALAN
STEPHENS
AN TALAMH
URNUIGH

14 - Types de Cheveux

```
U  D  L  F  T  R  G  E  A  L  D  J  G  A
R  L  J  N  F  H  O  T  X  W  P  M  F  U
P  J  S  B  B  H  I  B  A  A  Z  A  A  P
M  N  W  T  A  M  R  N  K  W  B  Y  D  E
G  M  Ì  N  L  D  I  J  T  K  R  W  O  R
W  Z  L  I  D  K  D  H  I  I  A  I  N  O
D  U  B  H  B  V  I  S  U  J  I  G  N  B
M  N  X  H  G  L  A  S  G  W  D  V  S  P
C  U  R  L  Y  H  A  C  H  Z  A  E  X  U
S  L  À  I  N  T  E  R  J  S  T  Q  K  K
S  O  F  T  Q  G  R  E  R  N  H  J  Z  A
C  U  R  L  S  B  V  Z  O  Q  T  I  S  K
P  L  E  A  T  A  C  H  R  Y  E  A  N  D
Q  N  Y  G  Y  I  Z  M  K  T  B  V  X  Y
```

GEAL	GLAS
BLAR	MÌN
CURLS	FAD
SHINY	DONN
BALD	THIN
DATHTE	DUBH
GOIRID	MFU
SOFT	SLÀINTE
TIUGH	BRAID
CURLY	PLEATACH

15 - Restaurant #1

```
A E F I S B X J A O Q Y S U
I R Y N A P K I N B I A G A
R M A T U I I S B C Y D I L
G E K N C N Q C G F M E A L
E A Q C E M B C Y K A S N E
A D C C C O F A I D H S C R
D H B Y Z L Z E R G B E L G
S J O Z Q A Y M Z I Y R À Y
N Z B T E D K G M G Q T R M
C B H X B H E X V T F C T J
F E L E A B D O G S K W A Q
M W A I T R E S S K T B I X
O W O R S G P E S L U T C X
J A C A C H I D S I N K E Z
```

ALLERGY
BOBHLA
COFAIDH
AIRGEAD
SGIAN
A ' CHIDSIN
DESSERT
SPICY
CLÀR-TAICE

BIA
ARAN
CEARC
MOLADH
SAUCE
WAITRESS
NAPKIN
MEADH

16 - Mammifères

```
K A U G R J T N V M F X W D
I A A P E J I Z E R Z U I U
M O N K E Y G E G A S Z M I
B O S G F Z E B F B C E X L
V R V Q A A R R N B Ù H H L
M H A R A F A E I B I Z E
L G X C F W O L F T F Z D A
R C W O T G X O G Y R O O G
C E W Y E L E P H A N T L S
Z A V O L I G B U L L G P I
Q C T T L O D E P J I O H O
K W A E R N T A U F X G I R
G O R I L L A R V I F S N A
E H Z E F T O O H K H P N F
```

- MHARA   RABBIT
CAT   LION
EACH   WOLF
CÙ   DUILLEAG
COYOTE   BEAR
DOLPHIN   FOX
ELEPHANT   MONKEY
SIORAF   BULL
GORILLA   TIGER
KANGAROO   ZEBRA

17 - Sports

```
P  X  S  G  Y  M  N  A  S  T  I  C  S  Q
Z  B  G  L  U  A  S  A  D  M  T  H  G  P
C  O  I  D  S  E  U  W  F  F  A  A  E  T
C  D  O  W  Q  V  M  W  G  V  G  M  A  Y
T  H  B  A  S  E  B  A  L  L  H  P  M  J
R  E  A  C  H  Q  C  U  F  T  A  I  A  G
O  I  A  Y  P  O  C  Q  V  S  I  O  H  O
T  R  Z  N  L  A  C  S  U  H  D  N  A  I
H  E  G  F  A  Q  T  A  V  A  H  S  E  L
A  A  G  H  Y  S  W  H  I  Y  F  H  U  F
I  D  Z  I  E  E  F  D  L  D  X  I  C  Y
R  H  X  K  R  N  W  W  F  E  H  P  Y  G
T  H  A  T  H  A  R  U  E  X  T  M  V  Y
Q  R  È  I  T  E  A  R  M  Y  E  E  V  W
```

RÈITEAR	GYMNASTICS
ATHLETE	HOCAIDH
BASEBALL	GEAMA
THATHAR	PLAYER
CHAMPIONSHIP	GLUASAD
COIDSE	DHEIREADH
SGIOBA	TEANAS
TAGHAIDH	ROTHAIR
GOILF	

18 - Chocolat

```
C O C O N U T U Z B J A I N
S I Ù C A I R Q K I U N N E
C O L A B L A S T T M T G N
C A R A M E L G T T P I R T
W Y S B L A S T A E Y O E C
Y M F L A V O R S R N X D A
B W O P E A N U T S F I I C
C À I L E A C H D Y Q D E A
G L P C A L O R I E S A N O
L F K A L D O S P U B N T Z
R E C I P E H Z J B J T N T
N M P S S W E E T M T I S W
X A X W X Q W H C E W O U P
Y N B D Q I G C J A L O R Z
```

BITTER
ANTIOXIDANT
COLA
PEANUTS
CACAO
CALORIES
CARAMEL
BLASTA
SWEET

MOLADH
BLAS
INGREDIENT
COCONUT
JUMP
CÀILEACHD
RECIPE
FLAVOR
SIÙCAIR

19 - Mathématiques

```
À  J  R  S  Q  J  R  W  P  Q  H  F  E  P
I  V  X  Y  À  I  R  E  A  M  H  A  N  A
R  V  G  M  T  S  P  J  R  I  T  R  R  R
E  S  Y  M  F  R  E  W  A  V  J  E  K  A
A  X  Z  E  R  Z  R  W  L  J  J  O  O  L
M  M  G  T  A  C  I  P  L  G  Q  F  G  L
H  C  I  R  C  U  M  F  E  R  E  N  C  E
A  E  R  Y  T  R  E  O  L  A  D  W  H  L
C  A  V  J  I  N  T  H  O  N  E  V  H  D
H  N  Z  K  O  U  E  F  G  G  C  L  N  J
D  N  V  T  N  I  R  X  R  L  I  H  E  J
J  P  O  L  Y  G  O  N  A  E  M  F  D  Y
T  X  T  A  Z  H  M  E  M  S  A  X  N  O
E  A  S  P  O  N  A  N  T  L  L  Z  Y  V
```

ANGLES
ÀIREAMHACHD
CEANN
CIRCUMFERENCE
DECIMAL
EASPONANT
URNUIGH

FRACTION
ÀIREAMHAN
PARALLEL
PARALLELOGRAM
PERIMETER
POLYGON
SYMMETRY

20 - Mythologie

```
U  I  L  E  B  H  È  I  S  T  F  C  V  Q
I  M  M  O  R  T  A  L  I  T  Y  R  B  L
B  E  A  C  H  D  A  N  N  L  W  U  I  R
U  R  N  U  I  G  H  C  C  U  L  T  A  R
M  N  E  A  R  T  V  Z  L  M  S  H  G  L
S  Q  P  N  T  Y  R  E  U  O  K  A  A  A
A  R  C  H  E  T  Y  P  E  R  B  C  I  O
Y  G  I  Ù  L  A  N  X  Y  T  F  H  S  I
I  G  B  A  F  M  M  R  K  A  P  A  G  D
R  E  V  E  N  G  E  H  W  L  G  D  E  H
D  R  A  O  I  D  H  E  A  C  H  H  A  M
E  B  I  R  E  A  E  L  S  M  N  P  C  V
Z  P  Z  D  V  G  R  Y  M  S  Y  J  H  O
Y  T  J  E  A  L  O  U  S  Y  S  V  Z  K
```

ARCHETYPE
URNUIGH
NEAMH
GIÙLAN
CRUTHACHADH
BEACHDAN
CULTAR
NEART
GAISGEACH

HERO
IMMORTALITY
JEALOUSY
LAOIDH
DRAOIDHEACH
UILE-BHÈIST
MORTAL
REVENGE

21 - Restaurant #2

```
O E B U I L E A N N E B A C
Q T O S X O X I O M H X N A
F K T F O L S O O E N R D T
D R J P A I Ò A D A C G Ì H
U I G H E A N N L S C O N R
B A Y S Q D Y W E A L B N A
A S A L A N N X S N P H E I
F G L A O I D H E A N A A C
D E I G H A H X C U I L R H
W A I T E R B P È S I R C E
B L A S T A S Ù I L P S W T
B W T Z E C O H C Z U O G O
G H L A S R A I C H X W O E
K D E O C H F F H Q Y I L N
```

DEOCH
CATHRAICHE
SPOON
LÒN
BLASTA
AN DÌNNEAR
UISGE
LAOIDHEAN
GOBHAL
MEASAN

CÈIC
DEIGH
GHLASRAICH
NOODLES
UIGHEAN
IASG
BUILEANN
SALANN
WAITER
SÙIL

22 - Couleurs

```
F R H W L H O B D U B H Z O
X K N B T H I D E O N Z O X
X W F U C H S I A I N M E F
Z : S A I D H E A N G N X A
S X W I S E P I A N E E C D
P P Q N Y K G F L T A R E A
I P E E O H J G W W L W A A
N U G U O X X L B U I D H E
K R O A R X I A O R A I N S
N P K U E G K S W L B S T K
Z A Y V D O H Y Y B Y Z Y Y
T I W J M R U O Y Q G B A D
B D T M N M E U R B M I X Y
S H H E I D X U R M E F I L
```

SPEUR-GHORM	DONN
BEIGE	DUBH
GEAL	ORAINS
GORM	PINK
: SAIDHEAN	RED
FUCHSIA	SEPIA
GLAS	UAINE
BUIDHE	PURPAIDH

23 - Avions

```
X T O G A I L I N F L A T E
C U A L T I T U D E L A A L
L I H A D H A I R J K H L T
N R Y A A P P D I T O N A U
E L D N Y R T G B U C E M K
I I R À I R D E Q O O O H B
N N O R N P A S S E N G E R
N G G D V A N K O N N F F B
S H E B Y O C Y F U A I C A
E R N H W O R H M R D G I L
A W K A Z O E D D B H U R L
N Q H I K V W P Ì L E A T O
P C D L T X Y Y S L E Z P O
E T H E A C H D R A I D H N
```

ADHAIR   TUIRLING
ALTITUDE   CREW
AN ÀRD-BHAILE   INFLATE
TALAMH   ÀIRDE
DÀNACHD   EACHDRAIDH
BALLOON   HYDROGEN
CONNADH   EINNSEAN
SKY   PASSENGER
TOGAIL   PÌLEAT

24 - Aventure

```
A C C Q W C D À I L L E U I
I H V O C U Ù R W G W Z L T
L E R X A N B P Q H N X L I
S A R S R N H P B U A S A N
D N R F A A A J O Y I D C E
F N A Z I R L X B G G X H R
D U D Z D T A L G A H O A A
E I J Y E A N E A U E T D R
A D N E A C L E A S A P H Y
L H V A N H R D J O C V N D
A E Y A T N X C O T H R O M
S F J Z Q U M W P O D U N Y
F P E X C U R S I O N T H T
D L E A S N A S K C K U N L
```

CLEAS	DEALAS
CARAIDEAN	EXCURSION
ÀILLE	ITINERARY
COTHROM	JOY
CUNNARTACH	NATUR
CHEANN-UIDHE	NAIGHEACHD
DÙBHALAN	ÙR
DLEASNAS	ULLACHADH

25 - Ville

```
S  R  T  A  I  G  H  F  U  I  N  E  M  B
S  O  M  A  R  K  E  T  A  I  N  N  Ò  O
Ù  C  C  L  I  O  N  A  I  G  Ù  R  R  O
U  R  N  U  I  G  H  U  P  N  V  Q  B  K
O  B  A  N  Z  O  H  E  H  Z  E  S  H  S
V  H  Y  R  Y  B  L  Ò  B  G  G  F  Ù  T
P  Y  Y  F  B  Z  J  Q  S  Q  W  F  T  O
G  H  P  L  L  D  S  C  H  T  Z  X  H  R
À  T  A  O  D  H  E  I  R  E  A  D  H  E
R  H  A  R  H  T  S  N  X  S  G  O  I  L
R  D  L  I  M  T  H  E  A  T  R  T  Y  U
A  L  O  S  G  A  A  M  T  Ò  W  A  P  J
D  Q  N  T  E  R  C  A  I  R  P  O  R  T
H  W  B  J  Z  C  G  Y  L  J  U  R  A  I
```

AIRPORT	BOOKSTORE
BAN	STÒR
TAIGH-FUINE	MARKET
CINEMA	PHARMACY
CLIONAIG ÙR	DHEIREADH
SGOIL	MÒR-BHÙTH
FLORIST	THEATR
GÀRRADH	URNUIGH
TAIGH-ÒSTA	SÙ

26 - Cuisine

```
Q  X  X  Y  M  B  Y  R  A  Y  J  I  F  C
J  N  S  O  F  I  T  U  G  W  B  V  W  A
W  V  P  L  N  A  P  K  I  N  D  Y  S  R
L  A  O  I  D  H  E  A  N  Y  I  V  G  B
B  B  N  J  G  Z  L  W  S  E  J  I  M  A
B  Y  G  P  R  S  G  E  I  N  E  A  N  D
O  O  E  L  I  C  O  P  A  I  N  P  R  P
D  W  B  O  L  A  R  R  O  A  J  R  E  À
W  V  A  H  L  F  B  K  J  C  N  O  C  M
N  E  B  C  L  B  O  V  F  Y  I  N  I  H
Z  E  U  A  F  A  O  R  C  J  U  G  P  A
C  H  O  P  S  T  I  C  K  S  L  B  E  I
D  J  U  I  C  E  H  D  N  S  S  L  R  N
C  V  M  Z  T  F  R  E  E  Z  E  R  B  N
```

CHOPSTICKS	FORKS
BOBHLA	GRILL
FREEZER	BIA
SGEINEAN	JAR
JUG	RECIPE
JUICE	CARBAD
LAOIDHEAN	NAPKIN
SPONGE	APRON
ÀMHAINN	COPAIN

27 - Gentillesse

```
M Q F I U E R U J F L C A S
H O V L V U H W X A A E O A
O S D K M S X Z E I O A F C
N P I H P L F J Q G I D R H
E I T B A A T E O H D A I U
S D F T U I G S E I H C E I
T A H H L N L L Q N L H N D
M L Ì O N T M X C N U A D F
O U O F J E H A P P Y I L E
E A R B S A C H X H M L Y U
K Y F E V C M S C I U M F M
O Z K N P H X V R W S T F A
A T T E N T I V E Q L Y Z I
I O M R A D H Q H L V A N L
```

LAOIDH   HAPPY
FRIENDLY   HONEST
ATTENTIVE   OSPIDAL
FHÌOR   EUSLAINTEACH
IOMRADH   MODHAIL
TUIGSE   FAIGHINN
EARBSACH   CEADACHAIL
CHUID   FEUMAIL

28 - Corps Humain

```
B  C  C  L  U  A  S  J  U  U  X  S  M  F
W  B  A  H  B  R  A  I  N  F  Y  V  U  F
C  T  P  B  I  Q  S  T  A  M  A  G  K  K
V  K  C  B  F  N  G  T  C  E  A  N  N  B
J  N  C  U  X  J  Ì  Q  O  Y  C  C  P  X
F  E  L  B  O  W  T  Q  H  N  N  U  H  S
G  E  T  P  B  J  H  C  A  S  G  D  K  B
B  O  A  M  H  A  I  C  H  R  X  U  U  E
R  N  T  T  V  W  A  A  Z  D  U  B  E  U
C  R  I  D  H  E  Y  O  E  F  K  H  Y  L
W  F  B  U  L  J  N  D  I  V  W  J  P  À
O  C  G  U  B  H  A  U  S  K  I  N  M
M  A  N  K  L  E  K  N  O  E  P  K  F  H
V  C  B  I  L  E  A  N  B  X  K  K  W  P
```

BEUL	BILEAN
BRAIN	LÀMH
ANKLE	JAW
AMHAICH	CHIN
ELBOW	AOIS
CRIDHE	CLUAS
STAMAG	SKIN
SGÌTH	DUBH
KNEE	CEANN
TONGUE	AODANN

29 - Épices

```
G  I  W  J  F  A  H  Z  A  O  B  Y  L  K
N  U  T  M  E  G  K  S  Q  Q  I  P  I  C
K  Y  I  Q  F  E  N  N  E  L  T  C  C  A
X  P  R  C  E  D  S  P  S  Q  T  Q  O  R
C  U  M  I  N  V  A  S  I  S  E  X  R  D
O  I  R  N  U  F  L  A  V  O  R  N  I  A
N  Z  B  N  G  S  A  F  L  U  B  P  C  M
I  I  U  A  R  A  N  F  J  R  W  A  E  O
O  P  A  M  E  B  N  R  P  Z  F  P  R  M
N  O  C  O  E  H  F  O  T  Z  N  R  G  U
G  H  Q  N  K  H  A  N  I  S  E  I  Z  P
C  U  R  R  Y  G  I  N  G  E  R  K  F  H
C  O  R  I  A  N  D  E  R  M  L  A  I  N
X  S  S  L  D  V  A  N  I  L  L  A  L  A
```

SOUR	GINGER
BITTER	NUTMEG
ANISE	ONION
CINNAMON	PAPRIKA
CARDAMOM	PIOBAR
CORIANDER	LICORICE
CUMIN	SAFFRON
CURRY	FLAVOR
FENNEL	SALANN
FENUGREEK	VANILLA

30 - Science

```
R T M È I N N I R E A N M X
U S Ì K H E M L A T H A O W
N C J R S E A L L A D H L P
A I D Y E T W I K R H I E S
T E R I U H J N B C Y E C U
U N D Y G K D Z C R P H U E
R T O À Y L X P H O O J L V
Q I B A T X U T E K T D E O
S S D T D A I B M U H B S L
Y T L O F O S S I L E V E U
E P S M T U B W C N S L S T
M O D H K H G R A V I T Y I
H E J Y H B T Z L U S A N O
F I S I C D B I G D D V H N
```

ATOM
CHEMICAL
TÌRE
DÀTA
EVOLUTION
FOSSIL
GRAVITY
HYPOTHESIS
LATHA

MODH
MÈINNIREAN
MOLECULES
NATUR
SEALLADH
FISIC
LUSAN
SCIENTIST

31 - Vêtements

```
N S P X C N V K J S E G S S
Z P W A D Q A A D Ì G L H A
O A Z E N E W H S O N O O N
L J G R A T C T A S Y V E D
W A M Q M T S Q L L S E W A
Z M A P A J E A N S B S I L
E A S C A R F R M I A A D S
P S B R A C E L E T P B O L
S E A C A I D Y Y P R L C T
F A S A I N X M S O O O T U
N E C K L A C E Q E N U O Q
C Y G M B A P Q R J W S R X
W J R Z L T V L È I N E N W
B H X A H W G Y Z H M V L S
```

BRACELET   SÌOS
NA H-ALBA   MAPA
AD   FASAIN
SHOE   PANTS
LÈINE   SWEATER
BLOUSE   PAJAMAS
NECKLACE   DOCTOR
SCARF   SANDALS
GLOVES   APRON
JEANS   SEACAID

32 - Arts Visuels

```
D E M A S T E R P I E C E W
E A F I L M L U E P E A N N
A S S L G V U X P A H T M V
L E E T E M I R E P L H C K
B L A I P N K H A B Q A W N
H P L R C L A Y N O D L I J
Y D L E I W J V T K Z A M N
A D A A J A V R A C H A L K
O M D C F X U O D Q U D X H
Y S H H G J A G H W O S W R
J Q O D S T E N C I L I Y P
D E A L B H C A M A R A O L
R D C R U T H A C H A D H R
C O M H R A D H F F B H F Y
```

AILTIREACHD	PEANN
CLAY	CRUTHACHADH
EALAIN	FILM
MASTERPIECE	PEANTADH
EASEL	SEALLADH
WAX	DEALBH-CAMARA
COMHRADH	STENCIL
CHALK	DEALBH

33 - Méditation

```
C S I F J E M O T I O N S P
I I O G L E K I N D N E S S
Ù T P I Q T L O N P E A C E
I P I D L J R X A D O W E S
N U B D P L E H T K F A Ò E
D C D O I R E I U E N K L A
A C H D A N A I R E Q E L L
T H O U G H T S R M I T F L
C E G L U A S A D E M T C A
H U A E B R E A T H A D H D
Ù O U G G O A V Y S U C C H
I H P O A I O M R A D H H B
S I M T P S U E X D Y Q D D
K C J X E G G L F N S F B X
```

ACHDAN   KINDNESS
AIRE   CHÙIS
CIÙIN   GLUASAD
SOILLEIREACHD   CEÒL
IOMRADH   NATUR
TEAGASG   PEACE
MIND   THOUGHTS
EMOTIONS   SEALLADH
AWAKE   BREATHADH

34 - Littérature

```
Q  F  M  E  T  A  P  H  O  R  M  R  A  D
M  Q  I  D  I  A  L  O  G  U  E  J  N  U
R  C  O  C  W  R  X  F  E  E  O  N  A  P
B  O  N  O  B  H  A  I  L  T  N  H  L  Q
Ù  I  S  D  S  Y  N  C  I  U  I  B  O  H
G  M  G  H  T  T  E  T  A  I  H  C  G  V
H  E  R  Ù  O  H  C  I  B  R  J  A  Y  F
D  A  Ù  N  I  M  D  O  D  E  C  I  M  S
A  S  D  A  D  V  O  N  F  A  A  C  Z  T
R  F  A  D  H  V  T  V  E  D  D  C  B  È
X  Y  D  H  L  W  E  R  Q  H  À  J  H  I
X  H  H  E  E  Q  Q  B  J  N  N  H  E  D
R  H  Y  M  E  C  O  D  V  H  I  H  N  H
K  M  Z  T  H  E  M  A  B  O  V  F  O  W
```

ANALOGY
MION-SGRÙDADH
ANECDOTE
ÙGHDAR
COIMEAS
CO-DHÙNADH
TUIREADH
DIALOGUE
FICTION
METAPHOR

STÈIDH
BEACHD
DÀN
POETIC
RHYME
NOBHAIL
RHYTHM
STOIDHLE
THEMA

35 - Nourriture #1

```
Y  S  C  F  S  Ù  I  L  Y  O  Z  B  J  D
N  T  B  U  I  L  E  A  N  N  U  A  U  G
J  R  Y  C  Ù  M  P  I  M  B  V  I  I  V
U  A  X  I  C  D  S  A  L  A  N  N  C  I
H  W  C  N  A  P  R  I  C  O  T  N  E  L
E  B  B  N  I  O  H  T  U  P  U  E  M  C
Z  E  A  A  R  Q  I  U  M  O  N  G  V  O
L  R  R  M  S  R  Y  R  U  L  A  H  I  F
M  R  L  O  N  I  O  N  D  O  H  V  Y  A
E  Y  E  N  M  S  L  I  A  S  A  I  D  I
A  I  Y  Q  M  O  E  P  E  U  R  A  N  D
D  K  H  Y  R  T  M  V  M  Q  H  Y  J  H
H  M  V  S  Y  J  O  C  Z  D  E  K  R  Q
C  U  R  R  A  N  N  K  Y  F  E  O  W  C
```

APRICOT	TURNIP
BASIL	ONION
COFAIDH	BARLEY
CINNAMON	PEURAN
CURRAN	BUILEANN
LEMON	SALANN
SLIASAID	SÙIL
STRAWBERRY	SIÙCAIR
JUICE	TUNA
BAINNE	MEADH

36 - Jours et Mois

```
S A N D Ù B H L A C H D Q D
I E N O D I C I A D A I N I
M P A T W J K K M Ì O S A M
Ì L B C Ò T R H M V N A N À
O A M J H G N F À E C T D I
S N W L P D M F R K G H À R
A L V Y G I A H T D Q A M T
C Ù L C D L D I I M Y I H U
H N O J Q U I X N O E R A Q
A A N G E A R R A N S N I C
N S A N T I U C H A R E R Q
M T Q X A N T S A M H A I N
S A A G H I B L E A N N J Y
E L A N T S U L T A I N R S
```

AN LÙNASTAL	AM MÀRT
A 'GHIBLEAN	DICIADAIN
MÌOSACHAN	MÌOS
AN DÙBHLACHD	AN T-SAMHAIN
AN GEARRAN	AN DÀMHAIR
AN T-IUCHAR	DISATHAIRNE
AN T-ÒGMHIOS	SEACHDAIN
DILUAIN	AN T-SULTAIN
DIMÀIRT	

37 - Championnat

```
C H A M P I O N S H I P P G
N A G E A M A N N A N T C L
L A O I D H S N A L C D U U
L Ì O G T K G M F X O R D A
C P E R S P I R A T I O N S
T O Q P A F O S R M L I M A
S K I P W D B V P W E N L D
N E I D F S A T A B A N L M
N U P I S G P I I B N L D E
X A L B I E X Ò S Y A E E I
C H A M P I O N R L D A E Z
A M B O N N K V S S H C I K
B U A I D H M N Z M G H M W
C K Q J Z U Z A Q X O D Y X
```

CHAMPION
CHAMPIONSHIP
COIDSE
SGIOBA
NA GEAMANNAN
LAOIDH
LÌOG
AM BONN

GLUASAD
COILEANADH
SPÒRS
RO-INNLEACHD
FARPAIS
PERSPIRATION
BUAIDH

38 - Pirates

```
B  U  C  Q  B  E  A  C  H  A  D  B  V  G
R  C  P  A  C  A  I  R  O  C  E  A  N  O
A  C  A  P  P  S  D  S  B  M  I  Q  N  L
T  B  R  Z  L  A  O  I  D  H  C  X  I  D
A  A  R  E  N  O  L  D  S  W  O  R  D  Y
C  D  O  Q  W  M  K  L  À  B  I  U  P  O
H  M  T  B  H  O  C  H  U  N  N  A  R  T
C  J  W  Q  G  V  E  I  L  E  A  N  I  F
A  I  R  A  M  H  A  P  A  I  V  C  J  E
X  O  Y  Z  G  H  I  O  M  R  A  D  H  N
T  R  E  A  S  U  R  E  I  C  N  C  M  D
U  A  M  H  J  Q  W  U  I  R  H  Q  T  E
S  G  H  I  O  U  R  M  C  U  N  F  S  Z
V  N  O  I  S  I  A  D  J  R  T  L  S  N
```

ACAIR	UAMH
DÀNACHD	EILEAN
IOMRADH	LAOIDH
CAPAL	BAD
AIR A ' MHAPA	OCEAN
NOISIA	GOLD
BHO CHUNNART	PARROT
BRATACH	COIN
SWORD	BEACH
CREW	TREASURE

39 - Activités

```
C F I G H E P E A N T A D H
L D A N N S A L A O I D H F
E A L A I N T U E F V S O A
A R C Z M C P A K A A T B G
S P I W M A Y N X I S B A R
J B H S N M G K D A H U I Z
S E A L G P P I T S I S R M
Q D Q K P A U P C G K G C E
H A K L Y D S Z Q A I I I Z
L L P A W H M D J I N L Ù U
Z S N S Q H H I N R G K I Q
I L E U G H A D H H Q L R P
B P H O T O G R A P H Y D H
S E Ò R R Y V Y S I G X M T
```

CLEAS
EALAIN
OBAIR-CIÙIRD
CAMPADH
SEALG
SGIL
SEÒRR
DANNSA
LEUGHADH

MAGIC
PEANTADH
IASGAIR
PHOTOGRAPHY
PLEASURE
HIKING
LAOIDH
FIGHE

40 - Fleurs

```
P E O N Y M W Y O P D A J S
O Z G L Y A N L I L A C J U
P E T A L G W V F U N V E N
P O H O M N M V K M D K P F
Y R U I B O C D K E E Y G L
Q C P D B L I L Y R L R J O
Z H S H O I D O Z I I G V W
M I S D U A S A I A O A M E
D D E R Q V V C I C N R W R
O I I U U O E P U S P D O X
R C C Z E D K Q E S Y E O O
H R Q T T T U L I P H N S L
J A S M I N E R I F O I Y Y
U G X J D H S E A M R A I G
```

BOUQUET	ORCHID
GARDENIA	POPPY
HIBISCUS	PETAL
JASMINE	DANDELION
LAOIDH	PEONY
LILAC	PLUMERIA
LILY	SUNFLOWER
MAGNOLIA	SEAMRAIG
DAISY	TULIP

41 - Nourriture #2

```
B R M G A E B B G C K P M T
P L U G H G N R F H N G A O
D S S P C G A O E R Q K B M
C X H J J P L C L U U D L A
E H R S T L M C K I W I M T
L P O J V A O O G T W U A O
E T O C P N N L M H B C N C
R C M C O T D I G N E I G W
Y E P M H L P A Y E I J O N
R A R A N E A Y E A G A H N
I R K P N K R T J C R S S W
C C Z P R K U R E H A M K G
E R B L G Y W B Y D P K B P
V N S E B A N A N A E O L X
```

ALMOND
EGGPLANT
BANANA
CHRUITHNEACHD
BROCCOLI
CHERRY
CELERY
MUSHROOM
CHOCOLATE
HAM

KIWI
MANGO
UGH
ARAN
IASG
APPLE
CEARC
GRAPE
RICE
TOMATO

42 - Océan

```
I  M  P  H  H  X  D  E  D  S  P  L  K  H
A  M  H  X  T  E  O  C  C  O  R  A  L  C
S  P  X  A  U  S  T  O  R  M  E  D  C  B
G  E  N  R  R  N  M  R  M  A  G  L  T  E
O  U  M  R  T  A  R  J  Q  V  B  À  T  A
C  J  E  L  L  Y  F  I  S  H  A  X  U  S
T  G  C  C  E  F  D  O  L  P  H  I  N  G
O  Y  S  T  E  R  E  S  H  A  R  K  A  A
P  G  Q  B  D  A  S  A  L  A  N  N  K  N
U  J  E  R  S  E  Y  Y  M  L  G  N  P  N
S  E  A  N  M  H  A  I  R  A  X  P  H  W
W  A  V  E  S  K  E  Z  C  N  I  N  K  G
K  T  E  L  D  J  Q  B  S  P  O  N  G  E
O  B  L  J  R  C  J  P  F  X  C  A  N  A
```

FEAMAINN	JELLYFISH
EASGANN	IASG
- MHARA	OCTOPUS
BÀTA	SHARK
CORAL	JERSEY
CRAB	SALANN
SEANMHAIR	STORM
DOLPHIN	TUNA
SPONGE	TURTLE
OYSTER	WAVES

43 - Remplir

```
C E N V E L O P E Q E M J B
U Ù Q N T Q V Y A F Y N R O
R T R A Y Y D T N P N K X T
O I J S V G P O C K E T X A
N Ù G B A S G A I D O O R L
B B J A P D U D S P Z Q B R
O U B G Q G R W X G O J H P
X Z C A B A R R E L A X À V
Z W B A N R D Z Q E Q N S V
B H M À I L E I D X W R A L
M E Q H R D L D Q M W K N J
D C J A R U T A R X S W Q C
C P N E L L E J L V C U V N
O V M G S R S O S U V Z K U
```

BARREL   POCKET
CÙRSA   JAR
BOX   BAGA
BOTAL   BUCAID
PASGAN   DOOR
ENVELOPE   TIÙB
BASGAID   MÀILEID
CUR   BHÀSA
TRAY

44 - Ballet

```
U R B Q C F G R A C E F U L
R G L I H H W H K O U A Y D
N T C C O S H Y F X V H O A
U E P A R G H T G U I S N
I C F T E D H H O T N O N N
G H L E O C S M J P S M B S
H N V Z G O G K M M T R U A
P I H P R M M W L C O A Y I
N Q C T A H E U Y P I D I R
Z U J X P R I G S D D H F E
C E Ò L H A D N G C H F J A
L Q I R Y D Q Y I A L R Q N
W H B I P H O Q L Q E E C I
O R C H E S T R A E S Q S L
```

CHOREOGRAPHY   MUSCLES
SGIL   CEÒL
COMHRADH   ORCHESTRA
DANNSAIREAN   URNUIGH
IOMRADH   RHYTHM
GRACEFUL   STOIDHLE
ON   TECHNIQUE

45 - Fruit

```
M  T  M  S  N  B  A  N  A  N  A  E  P  A
E  K  S  Y  K  E  H  A  R  M  D  P  I  V
L  R  V  K  I  L  C  M  T  K  J  W  N  O
O  G  U  B  W  E  A  T  U  L  T  E  E  C
N  R  R  C  I  M  W  P  A  P  A  Y  A  A
C  A  A  N  X  O  G  K  V  R  K  F  P  D
F  P  T  I  G  N  G  T  W  S  I  W  P  O
I  E  U  P  N  U  M  A  N  G  O  N  L  Y
G  T  C  L  B  S  A  V  H  O  W  L  E  T
C  O  H  N  B  F  Q  V  P  E  U  R  A  N
E  B  E  R  R  Y  O  M  A  Y  I  X  D  Y
A  P  R  I  C  O  T  A  P  P  L  E  K  E
W  R  R  A  S  P  B  E  R  R  Y  M  Z  D
P  C  Y  X  J  P  E  A  C  H  R  D  G  L
```

APRICOT	KIWI
PINEAPPLE	MANGO
AVOCADO	MELON
BERRY	NECTARINE
BANANA	ORAINS
CHERRY	PAPAYA
LEMON	PEACH
FIG	PEURAN
RASPBERRY	APPLE
GUAVA	GRAPE

46 - Surf

```
N A G A O I T H E O T F F B
W O R F N R D P E W U D O I
A T H L E T E À I R D E A Z
V O T M A Ò L J D A Z V M N
E U L S R I Z F E F A D G O
M H R K T S I Q C R O W D S
D V B U I E F J H S S W P T
S D V A K A E D A T E E W O
Y P Q Z D C B K M A F O Y I
F J Ò F A H X M P M B C L D
A X E R C A P H I A M E E H
C A P N S I R Y O G Q A T L
O A D G I D Z E N N U N P E
B E A C H H A I M S I R X Y
```

SPÒRS
ATHLETE
CHAMPION
TÒISEACHAIDH
STAMAG
ÀIRDE
NEART
CROWDS
AIMSIR

FOAM
OCEAN
BEACH
SEO
JERSEY
STOIDHLE
WAVE
NA GAOITHE

47 - Technologie

```
B Y T E S D Y Z C K L I H N
H C R U T H C L Ò A Y Q R G
R U F D À T A R H E M O B S
A R A È I S M X E K K A V C
B S I A S D M X B N S L R P
H O D N Y M S E L C P Z J A
S R H A V D A E U W X S B D
A L L M R S W S A S G R Ì N
I N E H A S A S F T Y C M B
R E U P B S B A K H A Q I L
O E A D A R L Ì Ò N Ì C W O
R A N N S A C H A D H O H G
F E A R T A T H A I C H R R
D J Z J B A T H A R B O G T
```

BLOG	FEAR-TATHAICH
CAMARA	BHRABHSAIR
CURSOR	DIDSEATACH
DÀTA	BYTES
SGRÌN	RANNSACHADH
FAIDHLE	CRUTH-CLÒ
EADAR-LÌON	DÈANAMH
BATHAR-BOG	MAS-FHÌOR

48 - Météo

```
U G V D Z P O S R H G A M T
H K Y U W D O H G B C S C E
J X V O O R T L A O I D H Ò
M K I O F O R T A U Ù M R T
I A Q O B U O H U R I S N H
L I R L O G P L T I N K M A
D O P B G H A U S O L Y O C
U A W F H T I R P M A A N H
R S B U A T G C F G L O S D
N H C G F Ì E L S H J V O J
U G E À R R A O T A O C O Q
I F H R O E C U O O I W N B
G O D E I G H D R T B K U S
H U H N S J L S M H N N C V
```

BOGHA-FROIS

CIÙIN

SKY

TÌRE

LAOIDH

DEIGH

MILD

TUIL

MONSOON

CLOUD

GEÀRR

MARBH

POLAR

DROUGHT

TEÒTHACHD

STORM

IOMGHAOTH

TROPAIGEACH

URNUIGH

49 - Châteaux

```
D A I N G N I C H D E W B C
F R T H A N X T L Y M S K L
T M N S W O R D P N P R L A
G O M O P B H C R A I Ì Ù C
O R P A R L Z R I S R O C H
E A C H I E A Y O T E G H B
D L O B N D V C N Y C H A H
T Ù R N C B R A N V V A I O
S W K P E M I T S R U C R G
D G N J B R B H A F O H T H
Y U I V F Y R A D S J D I A
A E G A B J L C L L R I S A
E R H F T U D H M L A F E K
X V T W Z H C K S V A N N Y
```

ARMOR
SGIATH
CLACH-BHOGHA
EACH
KNIGHT
CATHACH
DYNASTY
EMPIRE
SWORD
BHA FO

DAINGNICH
AON
BALLA
NOBLE
LÙCHAIRT
PRINCE
PRIONNSA
RÌOGHACHD
TÙR

50 - Randonnée

```
A  I  N  M  E  A  C  H  A  D  H  O  D  U
F  I  A  D  H  A  I  C  H  N  L  T  W  L
J  S  S  R  E  I  B  U  R  N  N  Y  C  L
I  U  G  R  G  R  W  O  I  F  V  G  L  A
Ù  R  E  Ì  X  A  Y  Y  O  S  W  Y  A  C
I  M  B  H  T  M  B  W  P  T  G  Z  C  H
L  O  T  K  R  H  J  R  N  U  S  E  H  A
Y  U  S  S  L  A  P  À  I  R  T  M  A  D
G  N  F  I  N  P  P  R  Z  W  W  E  N  H
M  T  Ì  R  E  A  T  A  I  M  S  I  R  H
C  A  M  P  A  D  H  E  A  V  Y  Q  C  S
U  I  C  F  B  I  D  N  A  T  U  R  Y  C
L  N  Q  K  G  D  E  M  X  S  W  Y  G  S
P  R  Q  E  C  O  M  H  A  I  R  A  E  H
```

AINMEACHADH	AIMSIR
BOOTS	MOUNTAIN
CAMPADH	NATUR
AIR A ' MHAPA	COMHAIR
TÌRE	PÀIRT
UISGE	CLACHAN
SGÌTH	ULLACHADH
IÙIL	FIADHAICH
HEAVY	DIDO

51 - Meubles

```
M H E S S B Z P D C S D J N
L A M P A R X I J A G R I M
R M T X F A J L P T E E A Z
D M G T Z T D L O H I S V E
D O K H R Y E O G R L S R O
T C Q D Ù E A W V A P E S Y
Q K Q L M A S Y Y I I R X A
A J R A H Z G S M C C J X B
O U F E A R D E O H H B U K
Y C O U C H D K L E E Q B R
N Z Y N T S L E A B A I D H
C U S H I O N S D X N P O C
U C Q S U Q N F H M G B W B
X S W U B D C U R T A I N S
```

FEAR	HAMMOCK
RÙM	LAMPA
DEASG	LEABAIDH
COUCH	MATTRESS
CATHRAICHE	MOLADH
DRESSER	PILLOW
CUSHIONS	CURTAINS
SGEILPICHEAN	BRAT
FUTON	

52 - Art

```
C  H  I  A  D  D  R  E  A  C  H  G  Q  A
O  E  B  I  R  J  Y  F  Y  J  O  I  C  D
M  U  R  N  U  I  G  H  V  P  N  M  U  P
H  C  O  A  G  U  J  Q  Z  P  E  O  G  U
R  R  S  I  M  P  L  I  D  H  S  O  S  T
A  U  N  O  Z  I  E  S  T  K  T  D  U  P
D  T  A  M  S  S  C  U  L  P  T  U  R  E
H  H  C  R  T  A  B  A  L  K  N  Q  R  A
V  A  H  A  K  M  M  A  O  B  N  K  E  R
M  I  A  D  N  N  X  H  H  Y  Z  U  A  S
M  C  D  H  Y  T  K  Y  L  F  A  F  L  A
O  H  H  C  H  T  G  S  X  A  F  S  I  N
B  À  R  D  A  C  H  D  P  U  L  T  S  T
X  R  D  E  A  L  B  H  A  N  Z  L  M  A
```

CERAMIC   DEALBHAN
COMHRADH   PEARSANTA
CRUTHAICH   BÀRDACHD
IOMRADH   SCULPTURE
HONEST   SIMPLIDH
MOOD   URNUIGH
BROSNACHADH   SURREALISM
CHIAD DREACH   SAMHLA

53 - Nutrition

```
N  C  C  F  A  X  W  F  L  M  M  K  B  A
U  À  A  E  Q  W  N  L  I  Q  U  I  D  S
T  I  L  R  V  G  D  A  I  T  H  E  A  D
R  L  O  M  L  P  B  V  B  I  T  T  E  R
I  E  R  E  A  A  B  O  V  L  E  Q  P  M
E  A  I  N  O  D  P  R  O  T  E  I  N  S
N  C  E  T  I  C  I  S  L  À  I  N  T  E
T  H  S  A  D  R  O  G  H  A  I  N  N  Q
O  D  W  T  H  Y  N  I  E  V  C  U  N  H
X  G  P  I  E  J  C  H  R  S  A  U  C  E
I  N  V  O  A  P  P  E  T  I  T  E  X  P
N  O  A  N  N  O  J  W  E  X  G  I  C  N
C  U  I  B  H  R  E  A  N  N  A  K  O  T
C  U  R  N  U  I  G  H  P  H  V  Q  T  N
```

BITTER	NUTRIENT
APPETITE	URNUIGH
CALORIES	CUIBHREANN
ROGHAINN	PROTEINS
DAITHEAD	CÀILEACHD
DIGESTION	SLÀINTE
LAOIDHEAN	SAUCE
FERMENTATION	FLAVOR
LIQUIDS	TOXIN

54 - Science Fiction

```
T S A O G H A I L T L V Q H
A E G A L A X Y K X E Q Q H
T M I D Y S T O P I A F N E
O Y M C Z P A M R O B O T S
M S A I N R F K V R H A E G
I T G N U E D E V A R S I O
C E I E T A Ò K N C A I N I
V R N M O D U L B L I L E N
P I A A P H A Y A E C L C N
X O R L I A À R K S H U J E
R U Y X A D C I H G E S Q I
S S K M T H W P R D A I L L
P L A N E T L J W D N O I X
F U T U R I S T I C E N T R
```

ATOMIC   IMAGINARY
CINEMA   LEABHRAICHEAN
DYSTOPIA   T-SAOGHAIL
SPREADHADH   MYSTERIOUS
ÀIRDE   ORACLE
SGOINNEIL   PLANET
TEINE   ROBOTS
FUTURISTIC   TEICNEÒLAS
GALAXY   UTOPIA
ILLUSION

55 - Vertus #1

U	H	E	X	D	M	H	M	M	W	C	S	F	P
R	C	E	F	V	E	O	T	O	L	H	H	E	R
N	J	L	J	S	J	C	D	L	W	U	F	U	A
U	C	I	G	F	B	K	I	E	M	I	S	M	C
I	N	N	E	A	L	A	N	S	S	D	È	A	T
G	U	M	A	T	H	W	L	S	I	T	I	I	A
H	S	W	S	O	C	I	C	E	K	V	F	L	I
M	J	L	A	T	I	S	E	O	U	P	E	S	G
O	P	U	C	D	M	E	H	Z	I	P	A	F	E
P	M	M	H	H	Z	A	G	I	K	Z	C	U	A
C	L	E	A	N	J	K	T	T	X	Q	H	N	C
C	E	A	R	B	S	A	C	H	D	H	D	N	H
E	U	S	L	A	I	N	T	E	A	C	H	Y	X
Q	A	P	F	Z	Q	Y	P	S	P	J	W	X	P

MATH
GEASACH
GU MATH
DECISIVE
FUNNY
ÈIFEACHD
EARBSACH
CHUID
URNUIGH

INNEALAN
MODEST
SEO
EUSLAINTEACH
PRACTAIGEACH
CLEAN
WISE
FEUMAIL

56 - Professions #1

```
N  E  A  C  H  P  I  À  N  A  N  N  P  G
C  O  I  D  S  E  K  R  C  A  U  E  S  E
D  D  T  D  O  C  T  O  R  S  R  A  Y  O
G  Q  P  A  E  Q  Y  K  E  Q  S  C  C  L
K  V  V  N  B  A  N  K  E  R  E  H  H  O
M  Z  Y  C  K  E  S  H  Y  U  I  L  O  G
J  E  W  E  L  E  R  A  F  T  M  A  L  I
F  A  K  R  T  U  U  I  I  R  Y  G  O  S
U  R  N  U  I  G  H  S  V  C  M  H  G  T
S  C  I  E  N  T  I  S  T  B  H  C  I  D
F  I  R  E  F  I  G  H  T  E  R  E  S  S
W  N  E  A  C  H  C  I  Ù  I  L  I  T  J
G  I  Q  L  T  O  S  G  A  I  R  E  G  X
P  L  U  M  B  E  R  Z  J  X  N  K  H  G
```

TOSGAIRE
NEACH-LAGH
BANKER
JEWELER
URNUIGH
DANCER
COIDSE
DEASAICHE
GEOLOGIST

NURSE
DOCTOR
NEACH-CIÙIL
NEACH-PIÀNA
PLUMBER
FIREFIGHTER
PSYCHOLOGIST
SCIENTIST

57 - Géologie

```
M  S  E  R  B  L  A  M  M  L  L  À  T  F
Z  È  T  N  H  C  C  O  C  P  T  R  B  S
M  O  I  A  A  A  I  L  A  V  A  D  H  A
I  B  Z  N  L  R  D  T  V  J  H  C  F  '
J  Y  O  A  N  A  L  E  E  U  J  H  F  L
C  S  N  N  P  I  C  N  R  I  S  L  G  E
P  O  E  J  M  D  R  T  N  I  K  À  E  A
W  K  R  A  U  H  E  E  I  M  G  R  Y  N
H  B  V  A  J  K  K  O  A  T  A  A  S  T
I  D  V  O  L  C  A  N  O  N  E  D  E  A
Q  U  A  R  T  Z  F  O  S  S  I  L  R  I
S  T  A  L  A  G  M  I  T  E  S  J  F  N
C  A  L  C  I  U  M  L  A  O  I  D  H  N
S  A  L  A  N  N  C  R  Y  S  T  A  L  S
```

ACID	LAVA
CALCIUM	MÈINNIREAN
CAVERN	CARAID
A 'LEANTAINN	ÀRD-CHLÀR A'
CORAL	QUARTZ
LAOIDH	SALANN
CRYSTALS	STALACTITE
MOLTEN	STALAGMITES
FOSSIL	VOLCANO
GEYSER	ZONE

58 - Cirque

```
T H I O G A I D E A N A S A
R A D M N G G M V M T C P I
I R V O C O L A P H I R È N
C W N N Q J R U K A G O I M
K J I K A K M M R R E B S E
E Q P E O J T K V C R A W A
L R J Y A H G J Q O K T K C
E I Y C S E A L L X G J W H
P B O W O B A L L O O N S A
H X N N O S T H Z O J L S D
A M A G I C T E G D Z J U H
N D I Q S L X U N L A U Q J
T J U G G L E R M T N C B R
Z L H Q C V E O K E C E Ò L
```

ACROBAT	LION
AINMEACHADH	MAGIC
TRICK	SEALL
BALLOONS	CEÒL
THIOGAIDEAN	SPÈIS
COLA	MONKEY
COSTUME	AMHARC
ELEPHANT	TENT
JUGGLER	TIGER

59 - Jardin

```
T E R R A C E Z N G R A S M
G D H Z V X S O S L Z I B G
A Q U D Q P G L G A R D E N
R A M F L Ù R B U S H A W K
A N L D F P T O R A O M P D
G R K D H E R N G C S U Q K
E B O I V A A P D H B A Z P
L A R Ù I R M N J U A D I Z
Y G C C N S P M S Q E R N D
I M H W E N O C O A W D B F
R E A K Q F L L O C H A N E
A T R E E E I Y R Q K M G A
K N D Q R M N N A G A Q K R
E V T B I T E W N M Q C C R
```

TREE	HAWK'
FEAR	SLUASAID
BUSH	GLASACH
FEANSA	RAKE
LOCHAN	ÙIR
FLÙR	TERRACE
GARAGE	TRAMPOLINE
HAMMOCK	ORAN
GRAS	ORCHARD
GARDEN	VINE

60 - Barbecues

```
N T O M A T O E S X H T D M
S A V U E N C J J G B O K G
T S G T E A G H L A C H T R
H T S E P I O B A R Y G M I
M S A L A D S A U C E H A L
C A H L H M S L H E R L M L
L M H X O R A N Y Ò I A Q C
A H D Z J W L N V L T S S E
N R M E A S A N N U V R B A
N A A M D W N S Q A Z A E R
S D S G E I N E A N N I X C
S H A N D Ì N N E A R C Z A
T I P V A L Ò N G O Y H U P
G Q D T U Z B O E R Y Q E Y
```

HOT	NA GEAMANNAN
SGEINEAN	GHLASRAICH
LÒN	CEÒL
AN DÌNNEAR	ORAN
CLANN	PIOBAR
AS T-SAMHRADH	CEARC
ACRAS	SALADS
TEAGHLACH	SAUCE
MEASAN	SALANN
GRILL	TOMATOES

61 - Anniversaire

```
D S S Ò K O V V W C S S P U
U O R X R T U Q H I R Q I A
M D R J L A T H A T S D E I
P Y C O I N N L E A N D J R
M Ì O S A C H A N F Z V O S
C A R A I D R P T D C R Y M
È O J Y G Y V U Y U Ò C F B
I G U Q A P P S G W G Q U L
C V P B S G J P I A J I L I
H A P P Y F V Ò F K D M K A
S P E C I A L R T C R H J D
Q W L U U G B S S L D N : H
G Z C A R A I D E A N B G N
C U I R I D H E A N K D P A
```

CARAIDEAN	HAPPY
SPÒRS	CUIRIDHEAN
BLIADHNA	ÒG
COINNLEAN	LATHA
GIFT	JOYFUL
MÌOSACHAN	RUGADH:
CARAID	WISDOM
ÒRAN	SPECIAL
CÈIC	UAIR

62 - Animaux de Compagnie

```
C  L  E  S  Z  O  Ò  K  M  G  Z  B  U  V
Z  A  I  G  E  W  U  I  O  J  R  I  A  E
N  V  T  X  Y  C  Ù  T  G  E  C  A  C  T
T  U  R  T  L  E  J  T  W  R  S  G  O  E
R  T  T  V  Z  O  S  E  O  U  I  E  W  R
X  L  I  Z  A  R  D  N  G  I  R  D  B  I
P  U  M  N  W  Z  D  N  K  S  G  Q  H  N
V  C  Q  A  P  Z  C  Y  C  G  Y  C  A  A
R  H  D  F  V  V  X  E  O  E  Z  Q  O  R
P  A  R  R  O  T  K  K  I  I  C  F  D  I
U  G  B  F  H  V  D  Y  L  O  H  K  G  A
P  B  T  B  G  F  Q  O  E  H  E  N  M  N
P  M  K  R  I  A  S  G  A  U  L  T  B  N
Y  A  Q  I  B  T  J  N  R  Q  S  U  W  B
```

CAT	LIZARD
KITTEN	BIA
SEO	PARROT
CÙ	IASG
PUPPY	AIGE
COILEAR	LUCHAG
UISGE	TURTLE
ÒIGRIDH	COW
RABBIT	VETERINARIAN

63 - Forêt Tropicale

```
O O F B M L I Y S I B D J O
D O B I I I U W I R O Ù T H
L E Ò I N F P A R Z T T Ì U
E B U E O B C M S A H R G
A M B E Ò V X P J H N C E S
S A Y V D S S H D S I H Q L
N M M Y B V P I F P C A P G
A A S M M F È B N J A S Q Y
S I T N L T I I N I L A K K
G L A U B D S A A E N C E S
H E L R R Y B N Y M Ò H M Z
P A Y K I M O S S F F I H U
Z N I N N S E A N W N F L P
O K B K S H I H E Y B Q W A
```

AMPHIBIANS
BOTANICAL
TÌRE
DLEASNAS
DÙTHCHASACH
INNSEAN
MAMAILEAN
MOSS

NATUR
NEÒIL
EÒIN
LUACH
DO
SPÈIS
III
BEÒ

64 - Insectes

```
A V M J P J E B Y E X D C W
Z P S Q Z Q H Q N Y U R V L
P J H D E A L A N D È A R N
Y J C I C A D A Y H O G B H
D Z I M D M A N T I S O O B
M M O O R H O R N E T N T G
W O R M J Q F L E A L F A S
X C S I C L L A R V A L I P
E S S Q H V Q O C T D Y G E
Q C A L U U O I D V Y T H A
C K A N L I N D P O B T T C
B E E T L E T H Q R U U T H
N E T D H D A O J W G I S T
N M E C O C K R O A C H D R
```

BEE
COCKROACH
CICADA
LADYBUG
LAOIDH
HORNET
SPEACH
LARVA
DRAGONFLY

MANTIS
MOSQUITO
DEALAN-DÈ
FLEA
APHID
BEETLE
TAIGH
WORM

65 - Ferme #1

```
U A G E H X F H B D A V L H
Q I C A T H A Y I V D R F F
W S S H X N I T S R O B E E
C E B G A O Y L O W N L R J
R Q V K E D J W N G K Z T P
C Q V I A L H Z R À E M I L
Ù V K U C A O S A I Y D L Z
J I M L H O P R M T K M I M
Z A Q C C G Y T F E A N S A
C F L D O H V J P A T K E X
L C R O W S E O K C Y J R F
F L O C C E A R C H G C I O
I W F W S K F Y F A K U C I
V K W Y A N P N N S G P E X
```

BEE	CROW
ÀITEACHAS	UISGE
DONKEY	FERTILISER
BISON	HAY
ACHADH	MIL
CAT	CEARC
EACH	RICE
SEO	FLOC
CÙ	COW
FEANSA	LAOGH

66 - Escalade

```
A M U C U L A I D H S N C S
C X A M H O G Q L S N E T E
B A M L W U B V E V A A E A
O N H O S C M G X Y K R U S
O À V K R J L H L H B T A M
T R È A N A D H A O Q X E H
S D D L E Ò N G K I V S O A
K B Ù T H I K I N G N E H C
E H B I I Ù I L E Q F G S H
G A H T A I R A M H A P A D
N I A U C D U C Z C C M L K
Y L L D T R U P B I K Z N C
C E A E Ò L A I C H E H G J
Q G N C H R U T H A T Ì R E
```

ALTITUDE
AN ÀRD-BHAILE
LEÒN
BOOTS
AIR A ' MHAPA
CULAIDH
DÙBHALAN
EÒLAICHE
CHUMHAING

NEART
TRÈANADH
GLOVES
UAMH
IÙIL
HIKING
SEASMHACHD
CHRUTHA-TÌRE

67 - École #2

```
L E U G H A D H C T F C L U
Y R A N N S A C H A D H E G
G U U K R F O G H L A M A O
I P À I P E A R V R R A B G
O R Z D Y P A C K A R T H N
N T E A G A S G L M S H A Ì
N V A J P E A N N A C S R O
S G R Ì O B H A D H I N L M
A K G M P U S N P G S R A H
C W J K L S J X P M S V N A
H G R À M A R P J M O R N N
A M Ì O S A C H A N R P V P
D L I T I R V A B F S O W I
H N A G E A M A N N A N F N
```

GNÌOMHAN
IONNSACHADH
LEABHARLANN
BUS
MÌOSACHAN
SCISSORS
PEANN
FACLAIR
TEAGASG

SGRÌOBHADH
FOGHLAM
GRÀMAR
NA GEAMANNAN
LEUGHADH
LITIR
MATH
RANNSACHADH
PÀIPEAR

68 - Antarctique

```
T  S  A  U  E  W  T  D  E  I  G  H  U  H
À  P  J  N  G  L  A  C  I  E  R  S  I  R
C  R  E  Ò  I  N  I  Z  G  N  U  S  S  R
O  S  A  J  E  Y  S  B  B  P  B  W  G  V
M  A  '  I  P  H  B  À  S  H  H  P  E  Q
H  I  L  M  N  T  E  Ò  T  H  A  C  H  D
R  D  E  O  W  N  A  D  A  O  I  N  E  L
A  H  A  L  D  V  N  S  W  P  O  F  R  U
D  E  N  A  H  J  A  A  Z  O  N  A  B  O
H  A  T  D  C  V  D  E  V  Z  G  O  D  D
O  N  A  H  Y  K  H  E  P  L  B  E  J  R
F  S  I  M  U  C  A  N  M  A  R  A  J  J
D  T  N  R  A  N  N  S  A  C  H  A  D  H
E  S  N  M  È  I  N  N  I  R  E  A  N  G
```

BÀS	DEIGH
MUCAN-MARA	GLACIERS
RANNSACHADH	MOLADH
COMHRADH	MÈINNIREAN
A 'LEANTAINN	EÒIN
UISGE	RUBHA
ÀRAINN	SAIDHEANS
TAISBEANADH	TEÒTHACHD
DAOINE	

69 - Professions #2

```
M E O Z T X X B C Q U P S G
A F L I N G U I S T R H U A
T E A G A S G O U I N Y R R
P R Ì O M H B L F O U S G D
T U R B D Q N O U N I I E E
E W Y D F Q C G Z S G C O N
P Ì L E A T A I X Y H I N E
W N R T R F K S U W B A B R
K C P E M H X T F G Z N Y D
H K P C E F H I A C L A I R
G Y D T R Z O O L O G I S T
K W E I N V E N T O R C J H
B N X V U K A L L L T K Z N
J E P E A N T A I R U D Z E
```

FARMER   GARDENER
PRÌOMH   URNUIGH
BIOLOGIST   LINGUIST
SURGEON   PHYSICIAN
FHIACLAIR   PEANTAIR
DETECTIVE   B'E
TEAGASG   PÌLEAT
INVENTOR   ZOOLOGIST

70 - Les Abeilles

```
B L B I V V S V Z M I W S F
C F L O W E R S J I S Y G O
Q T O C G H O Q E L M M I Z
A R S M L U S A N D O N A Y
B U S O I D Y C U G J R T E
H A O P G G I G W Q D T H S
A I M F E A R C I U I L A E
N L V M À R A I N N E A N Y
R L O E D D H V O B B R V F
I E U A G E C O S Y S T E M
G A U S E N D L E A S N A S
H D H A Q K S W A R M B V C
D H M N D I D O A B K W I D
Z L I S M B B E I X C C E A
```

SGIATHAN	ÀRAINNEAN
FEAR-CIUIL	DH'
WAX	GARDEN
DLEASNAS	MIL
SWARM	BIA
ECOSYSTEM	LUSAN
BLOSSOM	TRUAILLEADH
FLOWERS	A ' BHANRIGH
MEASAN	HIVE
SMO	DIDO

71 - Automne

```
A  I  O  R  C  H  A  R  D  R  V  N  N  R
O  H  P  À  R  X  E  V  H  E  P  A  U  Q
D  U  D  I  W  V  T  S  J  V  M  T  W  E
A  H  M  T  Ì  R  E  N  K  V  W  Y  O  B
C  I  O  H  P  C  K  F  A  P  P  L  E  S
H  N  L  E  B  N  A  F  T  P  C  W  C  Y
W  T  A  I  M  S  I  R  È  R  H  N  F  U
A  K  D  L  I  S  F  N  I  E  H  P  B
G  C  H  D  S  O  S  N  U  A  S  S  K  I
D  D  O  M  M  U  T  E  I  N  T  E  A  N
O  T  N  R  O  Q  L  K  K  W  N  U  N  R
E  Q  U  I  N  O  X  E  Y  W  U  T  R  E
R  P  I  C  J  P  U  N  Y  M  T  V  A  N
I  L  D  O  C  A  J  F  M  H  S  M  W  J
```

CHESTNUTS	MOLADH
TÌRE	MIS
EQUINOX	NATUR
FÈIS	APPLES
TEINTEAN	RÀITHEIL
ACORN	ORCHARD
AIMSIR	AODACH

72 - Conduite

```
P P W Q C S T B N A C G C M
E Q N K W À Y H A C Ò A E O
D K A M I B R O G O M R A T
E T S T B H V C A B H A D O
S Q R E R A V H O E D G C R
T R A F A I G U I O H E P C
R W T Q K L G N T X A U N Y
I B H O E T V N H H I L L C
A P A L S E O A E L L A G L
N G D A F A Q R P O L I C E
E P A Z S C E T U B A I S T
I C B S R H C O N N A D H Z
J P W L N D T U N A I L C L
A I R A M H A P A E E F Z N
```

TUBAIST
CONNADH
AIR A ' MHAPA
BHO CHUNNART
BRAKES
GARAGE
GAS
CEAD
CO
MOTORCYCLE

PEDESTRIAN
POLICE
RATHAD
SÀBHAILTEACHD
TRAFAIG
CÒMHDHAIL
TUNAIL
NA GAOITHE
CÀR

73 - Plantes

```
W K Y M P L P C P G R A S F
U L Y C B U F U S A P D Z L
F O L I A G E F O R E S T Ò
L À W V M C R T T D T C Y R
Ù M S Y B Z T R E E A Z I A
R O O T Ù Y I U B N L P R I
R S P I R H L C S U Y J X D
F S G F S V I I B C S T Q H
B E R R Y Q S B N W W H G V
G A X J X B E L A O I D H Z
V U C P U I R U W P B S R L
N S H H Y U Z D W X R N Z O
O B O T A N Y F A V Z L X H
S I M R D B E A N D L M L T
```

TREE	FOREST
BERRY	FÀS
BAMBÙ	BEAN
BOTANY	GRAS
BUSH	GARDEN
CACTUS	IVY
FERTILISER	MOSS
FOLIAGE	PETAL
FLÙR	ROOT
FLÒRAIDH	LAOIDH

74 - Ferme #2

```
C A H A Z G D M B A R L E Y
H N D F J E B U E A O M X Y
R T A S A Ò E T I A I M R B
U S B A N I R X Q L D N Z J
I A W I N D M I L L L O N I
T B V A T H L I T I R E W E
H H G L A S R A I C H A A R
N A K T R A C T A R A B T G
E I B I A C O I R C E B L L
A L I R R I G A T I O N L Z
C T U N N A G F M E A S A N
H A I N M E A C H A D H M Y
D M O R C H A R D M W Z A O
B G P R A T W F A R M E R X
```

LITIR	GLASRAICH
FARMER	COIRCE
AINMEACHADH	WINDMILL
CHRUITHNEACHD	DUILLEAG
TUNNAG	BIA
MEASAN	GEÒIDH
AN T-SABHAIL	BARLEY
IRRIGATION	MEADOW
BAINNE	TRACTAR
LLAMA	ORCHARD

75 - École #1

```
L E A B H R A I C H E A N A
Q I O F R L F T L W L U P I
Q I O R À I R E A M H A N B
H L P À I P E A R X Z P K I
E F U T Q M A T H B V H D D
Y T L I G U G S F H L T R E
K I W O D E A S G O Ò E F I
P E N S A X I L T A N A S L
L E A B H A R L A N N G T S
Y S A Q R M T S D Z J A F L
M M K N Y S E W P G J S N C
W T T Y N O A S V Ò T G F M
C K W Y U F N A C G R L C D
C A R A I D E A N V U S U H
```

AIBIDEIL
CARAIDEAN
SPÒRS
LEABHARLANN
DEASG
PEANN
PENS
LÒN

PASGANAN
TEAGASG
EXAMS
LEABHRAICHEAN
MATH
ÀIREAMHAN
PÀIPEAR
FREAGAIRTEAN

76 - Vacances #2

```
P  T  T  T  U  R  A  S  C  Y  C  X  A  K
A  H  A  E  J  T  Q  W  A  T  Ò  X  W  N
S  S  M  I  N  Q  R  V  M  R  M  X  C  Y
S  U  O  U  G  T  L  E  P  È  H  L  U  U
P  A  L  V  S  H  W  B  A  A  D  C  R  S
O  I  A  E  E  L  Ò  L  D  N  H  H  S  K
R  R  I  I  A  Y  P  S  H  U  A  K  E  M
T  P  D  L  R  L  Z  M  T  V  I  S  A  N
K  O  H  E  X  A  S  N  O  A  L  E  C  Q
G  R  E  A  X  O  M  O  T  K  C  H  H  B
W  T  A  N  U  I  Z  H  O  Y  È  O  A  E
B  T  N  Z  X  D  Z  G  A  W  I  I  D  A
D  E  A  L  B  H  A  N  T  P  N  T  A  C
T  A  C  S  A  I  D  H  P  K  A  J  N  H
```

AIRPORT	BEACH
CAMPADH	MOLAIDHEAN
AIR A ' MHAPA	TACSAIDH
CÈIN	TENT
TAIGH-ÒSTA	TRÈAN
EILEAN	CÒMHDHAIL
CUR-SEACHADAN	LAOIDH
SEA	VISA
PASSPORT	TURAS
DEALBHAN	

77 - Outils

```
H  V  H  T  S  X  C  B  S  H  D  H  O  S
S  A  I  D  P  J  U  E  U  G  V  J  N  L
T  X  M  M  L  F  I  B  T  A  I  G  W  U
A  R  T  M  I  T  B  C  W  B  F  A  S  A
P  B  K  O  E  F  H  À  R  A  D  H  N  S
L  B  Y  V  R  R  L  W  Ò  M  F  I  O  A
E  Q  J  P  S  C  E  L  P  U  I  E  M  I
R  H  W  W  S  W  H  S  S  P  B  Z  D
S  C  I  S  S  O  R  S  G  L  U  E  H  I
V  Z  P  X  R  F  J  Q  L  H  G  M  C  Y
M  D  X  M  A  L  L  E  T  S  C  R  E  W
U  D  W  U  A  Y  D  H  U  H  G  T  F  T
V  L  L  E  A  C  P  H  Z  A  M  D  G  H
J  V  O  Q  V  C  À  B  A  L  I  X  B  I
```

STAPLER	MALLET
CÀBAL	HAMMER
SCISSORS	SLUASAID
GLUE	PLIERS
RÒP	CUIBHLE
SGIAN	TORCH
FHÀRADH	SCREW
AX	

78 - Temps

```
U W K E F O G N V L M D M B
A R M Q K F N F K Q Ì E Ì L
I I N A N D È Y Q J O I O I
R S E A C H D A I N S C S A
X L B O I D H C H E U H A D
P M U S W G C L O C X E C H
M G I E Z L H A N I S A H N
I A D O M O A T Y C I D A A
T M D I N A N H J K I O N I
P P Z A Q A E A M H À I N L
D Z U O I E I N L I N N F Q
S U U H Q N L D O J M H D S
X J C L Y G N T A V D X U K
B L I A D H N A Y A B D T V
```

BLIADHNA
BLIADHNAIL
A-MHÀIN
MUS
URNAIGH
MÌOSACHAN
DEICHEAD
UAIR
AN-DÈ
CLOC

LATHA
A-NIS
MADAINN
CHAN EIL
MIONAID
MÌOS
OIDHCHE
SEACHDAIN
LINN

79 - Maison

```
F D G W Q C Y C N X U L L G
I P O S W K B U P Q R J E A
C U Z R N G A R D E N M A R
E B C A A E A T A V U A B A
I A D H F S N A T T I C H G
L L W G R L J I W N G A A E
T L Y R M A L N C R H M R A
E A O U N M I S Y J Z H L C
B R O O M P A C H D U À A H
E K M O L A D H H H O I N I
T E A L L A C H D E F N N D
F E A N S A P B U Z A T R S
S E Ò M A R M F D A R N U I
M U L L A C H A M L W J O N
```

BROOM	ATTIC
LEABHARLANN	GARDEN
SEÒMAR	LAMPA
TEALLACH	MOLADH
IUCHRAICHEAN	BALLA
FEANSA	CEILTE
A ' CHIDSIN	DORAS
A-MHÀIN	CURTAINS
URNUIGH	BRAT
GARAGE	MULLACH

80 - Légumes

```
B  L  D  M  F  W  O  J  L  G  L  I  A  C
R  T  R  U  E  G  G  P  L  A  N  T  R  E
O  V  M  S  A  S  T  S  P  E  A  O  T  L
C  U  T  H  M  H  L  U  B  U  R  M  I  E
C  P  C  R  A  A  R  I  R  R  O  A  C  R
O  D  U  O  I  L  Q  A  A  N  A  T  H  Y
L  U  R  O  N  L  Q  Q  D  S  I  O  O  B
I  O  R  M  N  O  A  F  B  I  A  P  K  U
H  L  A  G  V  T  C  Q  M  S  S  I  E  I
G  I  N  G  E  R  O  N  I  O  N  H  D  L
P  V  C  U  C  U  M  B  E  R  Z  D  I  E
F  E  P  U  M  P  K  I  N  E  E  F  M  A
U  N  Y  L  R  K  I  X  F  C  W  D  P  N
E  K  W  Y  M  P  A  R  S  L  E  Y  L  N
```

FEAMAINN	SLIASAID
ARTICHOKE	GINGER
EGGPLANT	TURNIP
BROCCOLI	ONION
CURRAN	OLIVE
CELERY	PARSLEY
MUSHROOM	PEA
PUMPKIN	RADISH
CUCUMBER	BUILEANN
SHALLOT	TOMATO

81 - Plage

```
N  W  D  I  D  O  P  G  B  G  S  F  O  N
L  A  G  O  O  N  E  E  K  T  W  W  N  S
T  M  S  H  C  N  B  V  Y  Z  Y  B  L  A
O  H  A  R  Y  Z  S  A  N  D  A  L  S  I
W  À  X  F  J  A  E  C  R  A  B  O  C  L
E  I  L  E  A  N  A  A  R  Q  O  I  L  B
L  N  C  I  Z  V  M  T  Z  R  U  B  F  O
N  C  B  S  A  N  D  I  N  K  M  K  Z  A
A  B  L  À  O  I  Z  O  W  U  B  T  B  T
S  O  D  W  T  N  G  N  J  E  R  S  E  Y
T  J  O  O  R  A  C  V  P  P  E  Z  V  A
P  Z  E  H  N  F  W  V  W  Q  L  Q  P  A
Y  L  I  L  R  E  K  E  J  D  L  K  S  A
I  O  C  E  A  N  G  O  R  M  A  A  F  Z
```

BÀTA	UMBRELLA
GORM	JERSEY
A-MHÀIN	SAND
CRAB	SANDALS
DOC	TOWEL
EILEAN	DIDO
LAGOON	VACATION
SEA	SAILBOAT
OCEAN	

82 - Vacances #1

```
M Y H N S A E V O T R J X T
Z D J G S M H N T U N P Q H
L A K E Q B R Q C X G G K I
B A C K P A C K D Q S E L O
P J X H O B X L J M J U X G
C M T A I S B E A N A D H A
L À U G A B E T Z P S A C I
A I R G E A D R A K B O U D
O L A U G R D A O S Q Q S E
I E S I E S E M G I W R T A
D I T I N E R A R Y N L O N
H D A D H B R A N N Z N M S
J N S L R U M B R E L L A Q
Q O E M S W W W F B R F N V
```

ADHBRANN
THIOGAIDEAN
AIRGEADRA
ROINN
CUSTOMAN
TAISBEANADH
ITINERARY
LAKE

UMBRELLA
LAOIDH
BACKPACK
TURAS
TRAMA
MÀILEID
CÀR

83 - Famille

```
I I B C P I U T H A R N A O
E K H O U A T H A I R E N K
M H R O A I T Q N P P P C P
S Q C G I K M E P N P H E S
E E L H R E A H R R S E S M
L I A A Q H T M N N E W T D
B N N N D N E À F E A Q O U
E I N H M L R T D Y N L R I
A G Q O X H N H W W A D D N
N H A U N T A A H Ò I G E E
O E J M V Q L I W Z R F J E
M A H I L W N R R J K V C X
R N A N T O G H A N W S Q P
F B R O T H E R X U R D Z X
```

ANCESTOR	MATERNAL
CO-OGHA	MÀTHAIR
A H-ÒIGE,	NEPHEW
CLANN	CUIMHNE
BEAN	UAIR
NIGHEAN	PATERNAL
BROTHER	AN T-OGHA,
SEANMHAIR	ATHAIR
SEANAIR	PIUTHAR
DUINE	AUNT

84 - Oiseaux

```
O  R  E  N  B  M  N  P  D  K  W  Z  S  R
W  S  E  R  F  L  A  M  I  N  G  O  K  W
D  P  T  U  N  N  A  G  C  G  O  O  S  E
V  E  O  R  E  S  Z  S  F  T  E  A  L  A
G  A  H  C  I  T  F  G  J  R  A  O  J  G
T  C  V  K  R  C  C  R  O  W  M  G  N  L
D  O  V  E  X  J  H  U  S  K  H  I  Z  E
S  G  X  Y  T  O  U  P  C  A  N  A  R  Y
T  T  W  T  D  K  T  X  E  Y  D  V  E  G
O  Z  O  J  T  P  H  U  A  M  I  I  B  M
U  G  H  R  V  G  A  N  R  O  E  P  W  M
C  V  V  V  K  U  G  H  C  N  E  M  M  A
A  A  M  M  I  L  P  A  R  R  O  T  P  Z
N  K  J  T  Y  L  P  E  L  I  C  A  N  I
```

EAGLE	EMMA
OSTRICH	GULL
TUNNAG	UGH
CANARY	GOOSE
STORK	PEACOG
DOVE	PARROT
CROW	PELICAN
CHUTHAG	PIGEON
EALA	CEARC
FLAMINGO	TOUCAN

85 - Disciplines Scientifiques

```
Q  B  E  C  O  L  O  G  Y  B  H  A  R  A
R  O  N  H  Z  M  J  E  W  I  S  J  O  R
A  T  E  A  A  K  E  X  B  O  T  B  B  C
W  A  U  I  T  P  Q  C  S  L  R  L  O  E
A  N  R  D  W  X  C  I  H  E  E  K  T  Ò
I  Y  O  H  M  J  Q  M  T  A  Y  I  I  L
R  F  L  J  G  E  E  M  W  C  N  F  C  A
N  N  O  K  C  C  O  U  J  H  B  I  S  S
A  O  G  Z  P  G  N  N  V  D  O  G  C  Z
C  U  Y  A  S  T  R  O  N  O  M  Y  Q  S
H  N  L  B  G  E  Ò  L  A  S  J  W  Q  D
B  Q  P  S  Y  C  H  O  L  O  G  Y  C  A
I  O  V  I  X  Y  W  G  Z  K  R  H  G  R
I  A  N  A  T  O  M  Y  C  B  W  G  D  H
```

ANATOMY	IMMUNOLOGY
ARC-EÒLAS	MECHANICS
ASTRONOMY	AIR NACH BI I
BIOLEACHD	NEUROLOGY
BOTANY	PSYCHOLOGY
NOUN	ROBOTICS
ECOLOGY	CHAIDH
GEÒLAS	

86 - Géographie

```
O  A  I  R  A  M  H  A  P  A  F  N  T  L
F  C  D  O  M  H  A  N  L  E  U  D  S  A
A  M  E  A  N  W  '  U  E  K  Q  B  A  B
D  T  M  A  Z  R  L  H  Z  S  J  C  O  H
Ù  B  L  Z  N  K  E  I  L  E  A  N  G  A
T  A  M  A  S  M  A  B  N  A  N  W  H  I
H  T  E  Q  S  O  N  T  H  L  L  N  A  N
C  A  R  I  R  I  T  U  A  T  H  F  I  N
H  S  I  T  K  R  A  O  H  I  Y  G  L  I
A  H  D  I  I  E  I  R  E  T  N  H  K  Y
S  J  I  X  W  W  N  O  T  U  C  I  T  Y
D  E  A  S  F  Q  N  C  Q  D  E  W  F  O
T  F  N  Q  U  K  P  I  R  E  G  I  O  N
H  E  M  I  S  P  H  E  R  E  L  O  X  K
```

ALTITUDE	T-SAOGHAIL
ATLAS	MOIRE
AIR A ' MHAPA	TUATH
A 'LEANTAINN	OCEAN
ABHAINN	IAR
HEMISPHERE	DÙTHCHAS
EILEAN	REGION
DOMHAN-LEUD	DEAS
SEA	RI
MERIDIAN	CITY

87 - Danse

```
P  À  I  R  T  M  C  G  I  N  N  H  M  U
C  H  B  F  P  P  C  O  L  M  V  E  I  F
L  U  U  C  J  W  E  U  M  U  T  Q  O  Y
A  I  L  B  P  Q  Ò  D  N  H  A  E  M  Z
S  W  D  T  N  C  L  Z  F  C  R  S  R  W
S  Q  U  H  A  N  G  W  K  U  H  A  A  T
I  O  W  Y  M  R  D  P  N  L  Y  J  D  D
C  N  O  Z  A  V  A  J  E  T  T  T  H  H
A  G  R  A  C  E  L  I  A  A  H  Q  G  B
L  H  J  J  O  Y  F  U  L  R  M  R  E  X
T  R  A  I  D  I  S  E  A  N  T  A  L  E
J  A  C  A  D  A  M  A  I  D  H  P  R  S
L  È  I  R  S  I  N  N  I  V  Z  Y  X
C  H  O  R  E  O  G  R  A  P  H  Y  L  N
```

ACADAMAIDH	GRACE
EALAIN	JOYFUL
CHOREOGRAPHY	GLUASAD
CLASSICAL	CEÒL
COMHRADH	PÀIRT
CULTAR	RHYTHM
CULTARAIL	TRAIDISEANTA
IOMRADH	LÈIRSINN

88 - Bâtiments

```
I D B T A I G H Ò S T A W N
C H Ù M Ò R B H Ù T H M E E
I E T S N Y H T E N T P N B
N I H W B O X Ù S R G C Z R
E R O O B S E R V A T O R Y
M E B R L G À M T A K W C O
A A R F S O R M B G G C A S
A D A L F I O T V A G A B P
C H C R A L S Y H R S I I I
W O H L G T U B P A Y S N D
T H E A T R H A E G Q T Y A
U R N U I G H A A E O E F L
N S A R A N T S A B H A I L
F A C T A R A I D H J L G F
```

EMBASSY
ÀROS
BÙTH-OBRACH
CABIN
CAISTEAL
CINEMA
SGOIL
GARAGE
AN T-SABHAIL
OSPIDAL

TAIGH-ÒSTA
LATHA
OBSERVATORY
DHEIREADH
MÒR-BHÙTH
TENT
THEATR
TÙR
URNUIGH
FACTARAIDH

89 - Pêche

```
U  J  F  K  J  E  K  B  A  S  G  A  I  D
N  È  H  F  A  Y  S  B  B  À  T  A  O  E
J  B  I  O  W  T  B  E  H  Y  X  W  X  X
H  M  C  R  O  P  N  A  A  A  A  S  D  A
F  M  H  N  V  K  S  C  I  X  Q  V  Z  G
W  L  A  K  E  K  E  H  N  T  O  G  G  G
D  Y  N  E  T  F  U  R  N  U  I  G  H  E
L  P  S  N  Q  E  I  J  G  I  N  I  O  R
O  C  E  A  N  W  S  D  V  I  O  L  U  A
K  O  U  Y  F  Y  G  W  L  Q  P  L  M  T
Y  O  S  O  U  P  E  R  F  E  K  S  C  I
A  K  A  E  Q  V  E  V  O  O  D  B  U  O
Z  G  N  A  A  K  A  Y  O  Q  T  C  P  N
D  Y  H  B  V  S  A  Z  Z  T  V  P  H  T
```

BAIT	ABHAINN
BÀTA	LAKE
GILLS	JAW
HOOK	OCEAN
COOK	BASGAID
UISGE	BEACH
EXAGGERATION	URNUIGH
UÈIR	SEUSAN

90 - Activités et Loisirs

```
U  W  B  Z  H  W  T  G  O  I  L  F  R  I
B  R  D  F  K  M  E  A  L  A  I  N  P  A
C  O  N  Z  O  B  A  S  E  B  A  L  L  S
U  A  X  U  R  T  N  V  M  G  P  D  U  G
S  O  M  I  I  V  A  I  B  T  E  U  Y  A
L  A  E  P  N  G  S  Q  I  X  A  J  R  I
N  N  H  T  A  G  H  I  K  I  N  G  N  R
Q  Z  C  O  F  D  K  L  U  Y  T  A  O  T
J  D  V  M  T  T  H  A  T  H  A  R  C  E
V  O  L  L  E  Y  B  A  L  L  D  L  H  A
J  W  O  F  K  V  G  L  A  X  H  L  D  G
C  U  R  S  E  A  C  H  A  D  A  N  V  A
O  H  R  U  M  K  U  R  I  I  Y  W  F  S
C  Q  W  M  X  E  M  E  W  O  K  E  U  G
```

EALAIN   PEANTADH
BASEBALL   IASGAIR
THATHAR   HIKING
BOXING   URNUIGH
CAMPADH   TEANAS
GOILF   VOLLEYBALL
NOCHD   TEAGASG
CUR-SEACHADAN

91 - Livres

```
G M N A C T U B V S P Q P D
Q C C D O F C À I I A D L A
G U V Z T W V R R N G U T O
I O M C H A I D H V E M L N
S D E F E W E A H E V U A N
L U D A A V Y C N N D X E A
I A À D C N G H S T È I D H
T L N À S H O D M I X O S R
I I A N A Q D B P V T E R E
R T C C L B W R H E L U A A
H Y H S B Q B X A A Q H I D
R V D Ù G H D A R I I T T E
S G E U L A C H D A D L H R
F N A U Y Y C U H U N H M T
```

ÙGHDAR
DÀNACHD
CO-THEACSA
DUALITY
GU
SGEULACHD
EACHDRAIDH
DAONNA
INVENTIVE

READER
LITIR
STÈIDH
PAGE
IOMCHAIDH
DÀN
BÀRDACHD
NOBHAIL
SRAITH

92 - Pays #2

```
D A P K P Z M P L S R L I S
K I V V X S A G Z Z C À A O
E K A Y E M E N P S C T P M
N G N M M Q C A A Ì P H A À
Y T R L E A B A N O N O N I
A N U K X U B T F N P S E L
È F I S I G G H H A A M O I
L I S P C R C A R L C D H A
G U R Y O A C I A B A K G H
L N Z I A I M T I À S T W E
T K P G N N B I N I T T B T
S U D A N N U Y G N A P F Q
U N N Y T I N N D I N N S E
P U A N D A N M H A I R C R
```

ALBÀINIA
SÌONA
AN DANMHAIRC
NA
AN FHRAING
HAITI
INND INNSE
ÈIRINN
DIAMEUGA
IAPAN

KENYA
LÀTHOS
LEABANON
MEXICO
PACASTAN
AN RUIS
SOMÀILIA
SUDAN
YEMEN
UGRAIN

93 - Fournitures d'Art

```
B  P  H  A  C  O  B  P  G  A  X  V  V  Q
E  R  M  C  L  L  C  S  E  Q  R  U  M  C
A  Q  G  R  À  A  A  X  E  N  V  Z  Q  B
C  O  Z  Y  R  O  T  Y  R  A  C  U  C  R
H  J  G  L  U  E  H  P  A  K  A  I  N  U
D  L  J  I  P  A  R  À  S  T  M  S  L  I
A  N  S  C  D  Y  A  I  E  V  A  G  L  S
N  S  D  L  H  Y  I  P  R  K  R  E  E  E
Y  E  S  D  A  Q  C  E  B  B  A  H  C  A
Z  U  U  V  A  J  H  A  I  X  S  M  Y  N
M  Q  T  W  A  T  E  R  C  O  L  O  R  S
I  N  C  D  U  B  H  E  A  S  E  L  V  U
X  Q  C  R  U  T  H  A  C  H  A  D  H  Z
F  U  R  O  T  N  J  S  N  B  H  J  J  Z
```

ACRYLIC
WATERCOLORS
CLAY
BRUISEAN
CAMARA
CATHRAICHE
EASEL
GLUE
DATHAN

PENCILS
CRUTHACHADH
UISGE
INC DUBH
ERASER
OLA
BEACHDAN
PÀIPEAR
CLÀR

94 - Jouets

```
T  Z  U  U  D  B  X  F  R  E  L  V  R  J
À  K  L  À  R  A  I  D  H  Y  V  V  O  A
I  T  N  D  U  L  R  G  V  E  E  K  T  D
L  C  Q  A  M  L  N  J  M  X  M  D  H  H
E  V  Z  M  A  C  M  E  A  N  M  N  A  B
A  O  B  A  I  R  C  I  Ù  I  R  D  I  R
S  G  L  K  C  A  L  C  L  A  Y  O  R  A
G  A  N  C  H  T  R  È  A  N  U  D  Q  N
K  I  T  E  E  C  U  A  R  B  K  O  V  N
W  I  K  F  A  D  À  F  T  O  À  L  L  F
X  N  X  A  N  V  L  R  Y  H  B  T  V  L
N  A  G  E  A  M  A  N  N  A  N  O  A  H
T  Ò  I  M  H  S  E  A  C  H  A  N  T  U
L  E  A  B  H  R  A  I  C  H  E  A  N  J
```

CLAY   NA GEAMANNAN
OBAIR-CIÙIRD   LEABHRAICHEAN
ADHBRANN   DOL
BALL   TÒIMHSEACHAN
BÀTA   ROBOT
LÀRAIDH   DRUMAICHEAN
KITE   TRÈAN
TÀILEASG   ROTHAIR
MAC-MEANMNA   CÀR

95 - Eau

```
C  I  R  R  I  G  A  T  I  O  N  V  K  M
A  M  H  À  I  N  T  F  I  W  F  B  Q  E
N  A  G  E  W  X  Y  L  B  P  I  B  I  A
À  R  W  A  V  E  S  O  K  X  X  N  L  S
L  B  M  B  L  M  D  D  I  G  T  M  L  A
M  H  Q  R  A  K  B  I  K  X  W  F  D  D
L  O  C  E  A  N  K  Z  P  F  M  A  F  H
A  D  N  Z  V  A  R  T  S  S  O  Z  D  Z
K  B  B  S  T  U  I  L  M  D  D  L  V  I
E  P  H  L  O  H  Z  J  Ù  S  E  M  C  F
I  W  W  A  P  O  J  F  I  M  O  I  S  T
L  D  W  I  I  I  N  M  D  V  C  O  G  O
L  F  D  C  S  N  O  W  I  R  P  T  R  H
C  G  W  H  T  E  N  G  E  Y  S  E  R  G
```

CANÀL	IRRIGATION
A-MHÀIN	LAKE
MEASADH	MONSOON
ABHAINN	SNOW
GEYSER	OCEAN
DEIGH	MARBH
MOIST	WAVES
TUIL	SMÙID

96 - Paysages

```
Z A F S Y C K W B G O M R O
Z B G A W E L W E L B J A F
O H O B Y A O I A A C M B U
Q A H U U N M E C C T M F O
L I S I F G W P H I W R O V
X N F I X L W I C E B E R G
S N W M S A A R F R K Y X M
H H P S U I T V A L L E Y O
T I R E A C E G O Z M I L U
Y E L A M H R E O O V L D N
C W Y L H E F Y D E S E R T
R U B H A A A S C N G A R A
C L A K E N L E G M K N F I
T U N D R A L R B E E D L N
```

WATERFALL	LAKE
HILL	SWAMP
DESERT	SEA
CEANGLAICHEAN	MOUNTAIN
ABHAINN	OASIS
GEYSER	RUBHA
GLACIER	BEACH
UAMH	TUNDRA
ICEBERG	VALLEY
EILEAN	

97 - Nombres

```
D Y S Y N Z C C N G Z C R Y
S E V P V N E Ò E O G W G P
E X I E I A I I O O C O Y O
A D À C Y O T G N Z H O C E
C H H T H I H S I X T E E N
H X I A N C I Z I H R F I O
D Q Z C X L R H T A Ì U T C
S E A C H D D E U G D D H H
T R Ì D E C I M A L E E I D
F I C H E A D H K Y U U R A
S H S D Z H X C T J G G D U
D H À D H E U G G J S A E F
S Y L M E I G H T E E N U L
N A O I D E U G Z Z O M G I
```

CÒIG
DÀ
DECIMAL
DEICH
EIGHTEEN
NAOI-DEUG
SEACHD-DEUG
DHÀ-DHEUG
OCHD
NAOI

CEITHIR-DEUG
CEITHIR
DEUG AN
SIXTEEN
SEACHD
SIA
TRÌ-DEUG
TRÌ
FICHEAD
NEONI

98 - Nature

```
I A X T D M E B S I O S H Y
R I A R C U B N E Z V E A Y
W N R O H F X W U Q Z R B Q
B M T P U F O L I A G E H F
F E A A L D W R N E D N A B
A A C I T E G H E G E E I E
S C H G A S J W Ò S A B N O
G H Y E R E C E I N T L N T
A A X A A R N H L O A Y À H
D D Y C I T B E A N M K I A
H H H H L U P Q X S A G L I
S A N C T U A R Y B C A L L
F I A D H A I C H D H I E A
G L A C I E R C G N R Z I X
```

BEAN   FOREST
FASGADH   GLACIER
AINMEACHADH   NEÒIL
ARTACH   CHULTARAIL
ÀILLE   SANCTUARY
DESERT   FIADHAICH
BEOTHAIL   SERENE
FOLIAGE   TROPAIGEACH
ABHAINN   DEATAMACH

99 - Bateaux

```
E  O  G  L  N  S  E  S  D  J  E  R  M  C
I  C  F  I  X  G  A  S  A  C  A  I  R  F
N  E  E  B  B  G  D  Z  O  I  S  N  C  T
N  A  R  S  E  A  O  A  S  K  L  A  K  E
S  N  R  T  S  X  C  R  C  A  N  O  E  Y
E  C  Y  Q  A  F  K  P  B  Y  M  L  R  A
A  F  M  K  S  B  U  O  Y  A  A  K  A  C
N  B  C  I  A  A  H  B  I  K  S  K  Z  H
C  H  E  R  V  Q  A  A  R  L  T  A  Z  T
R  I  M  I  Ò  U  R  R  I  À  X  W  G  W
E  S  O  X  R  P  S  A  P  N  K  I  G  T
W  W  A  V  E  S  Y  F  C  G  N  U  I  Y
M  U  N  Y  D  H  T  T  B  O  M  Q  M  O
S  A  I  L  B  O  A  T  E  S  B  K  P  H
```

ACAIR	- LÀN
BUOY	SAILOR
CANOE	MAST
RÒP	SEA
DOC	EINNSEAN
CREW	OCEAN
FERRY	RAFT
ABHAINN	WAVES
KAYAK	SAILBOAT
LAKE	YACHT

100 - Mesures

```
B E U W W J O G C B N F À R
A R Y L N Z Q R E O A C I B
I O N A D J R A U V G M R M
D R K Ò E K J M M Q V Y D I
H D B I C I K H W Q F Q E O
T X R R I L G E Q I A D C N
O O V L M O O A B H I T H A
N U M E A G N T K X D S J I
I R N A L R F A C L X Y Z D
H N U C D A G I X I N G Z L
K U E H E M D R O T K Z C E
K I L O M E T E R I K Z O U
N G N L X T Z V C R A Z W D
R H F B Z A S F S Z T O V B
```

IONAD	TOMAD
CEUM	MHEATAIR
DECIMAL	MIONAID
GRAM	BAIDHT
ÀIRDE	OUNCE
KILOGRAM	URNUIGH
KILOMETER	ÒIRLEACH
LEUD	A BHITH A
LITIR	TON
FAID	

1 - Été

2 - Adjectifs #2

3 - Formes

4 - Salle de Bains

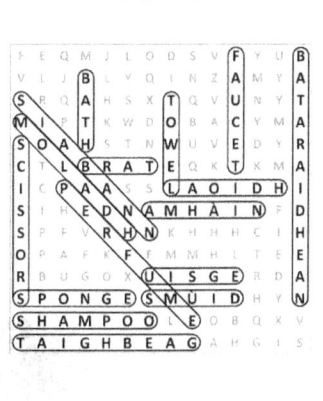

5 - Adjectifs #1

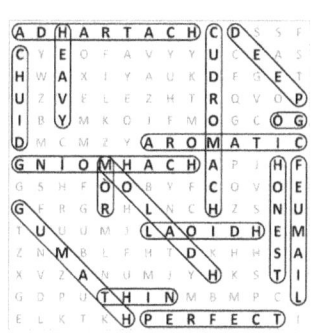

6 - Instruments de Musique

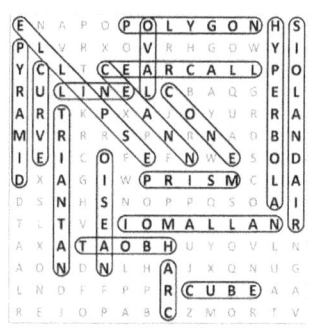

7 - Échecs

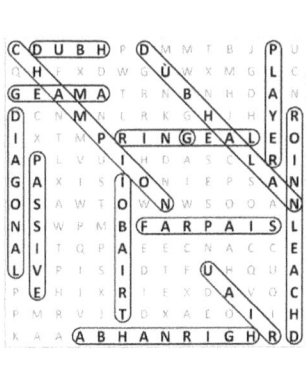

8 - Herboristerie

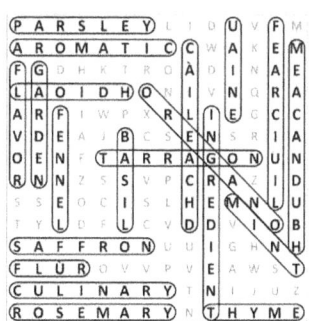

9 - Véhicules

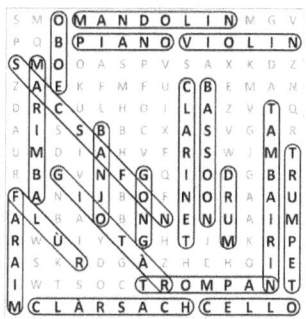

10 - Camping

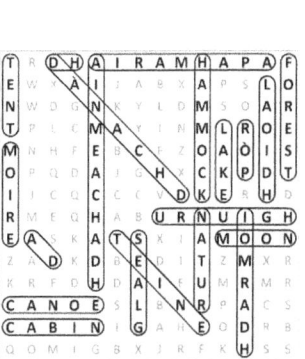

11 - Conservation

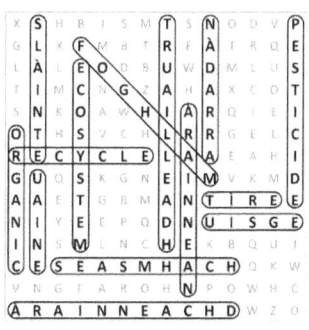

12 - Écologie

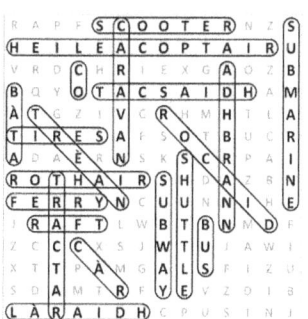
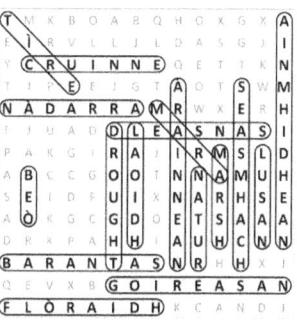

13 - Astronomie

14 - Types de Cheveux

15 - Restaurant #1

16 - Mammifères

17 - Sports

18 - Chocolat

19 - Mathématiques

20 - Mythologie

21 - Restaurant #2

22 - Couleurs

23 - Avions

24 - Aventure

25 - Ville
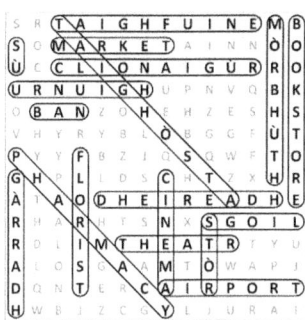

26 - Cuisine
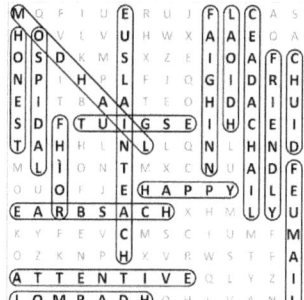

27 - Gentillesse

28 - Corps Humain
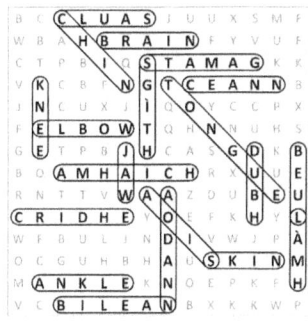

29 - Épices
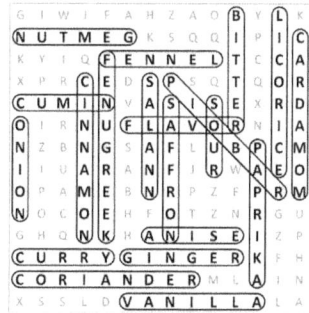

30 - Science
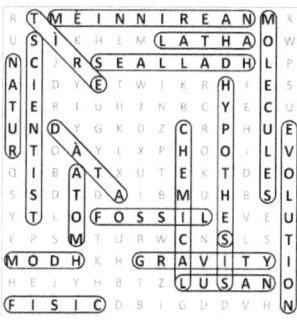

31 - Vêtements
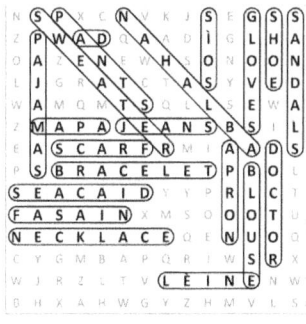

32 - Arts Visuels
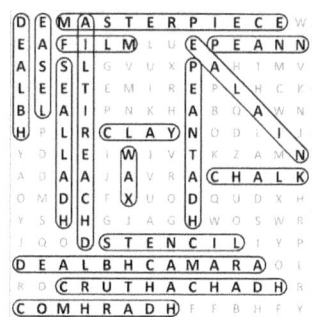

33 - Méditation
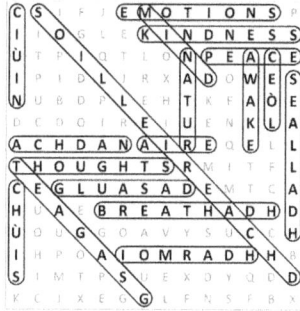

34 - Littérature
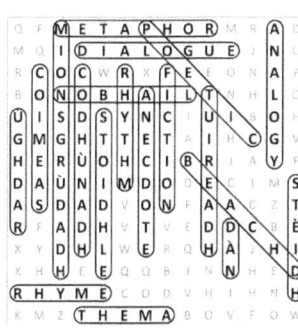

35 - Nourriture #1
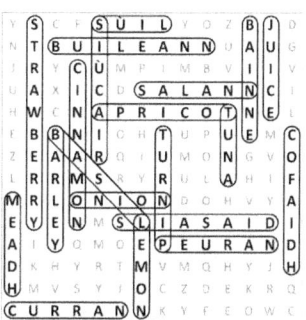

36 - Jours et Mois

37 - Championnat

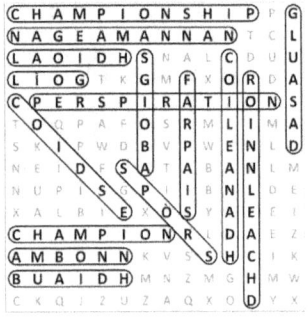

38 - Pirates

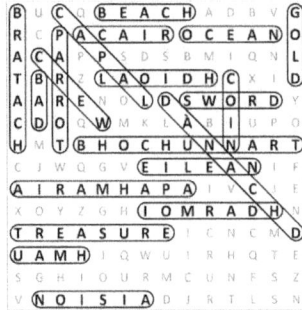

39 - Activités

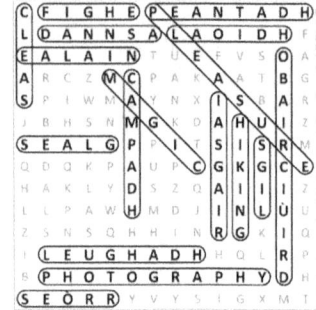

40 - Fleurs

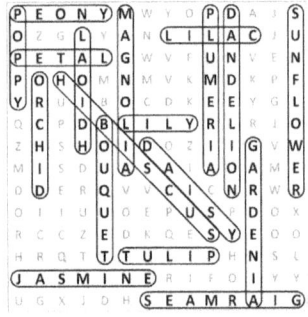

41 - Nourriture #2

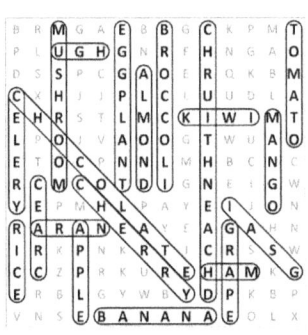

42 - Océan

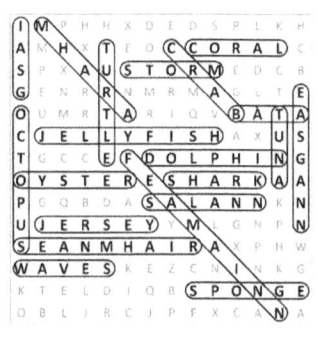

43 - Remplir

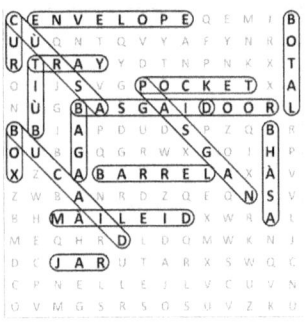

44 - Ballet

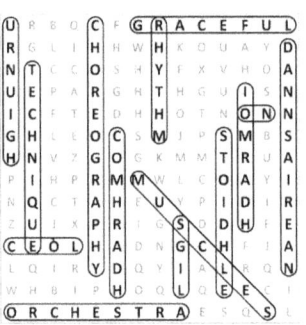

45 - Fruit

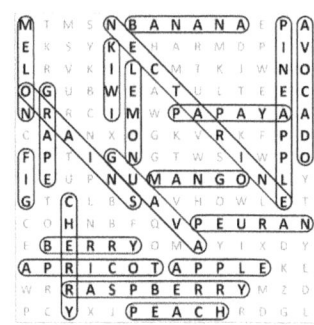

46 - Surf

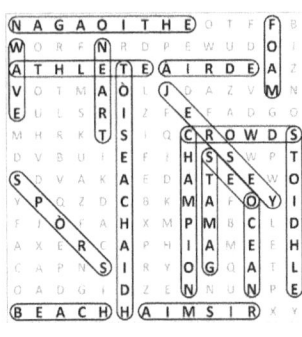

47 - Technologie

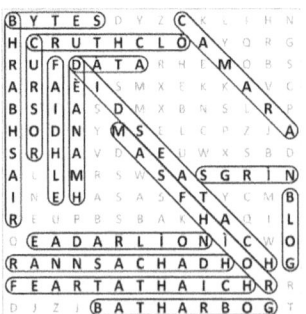

48 - Météo

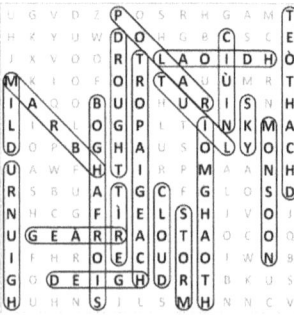

49 - Châteaux

50 - Randonnée

51 - Meubles

52 - Art

53 - Nutrition

54 - Science Fiction

55 - Vertus #1

56 - Professions #1

57 - Géologie

58 - Cirque

59 - Jardin

60 - Barbecues

61 - Anniversaire

62 - Animaux de Compagnie

63 - Forêt Tropicale

64 - Insectes

65 - Ferme #1

66 - Escalade

67 - École #2

68 - Antarctique

69 - Professions #2

70 - Les Abeilles

71 - Automne

72 - Conduite

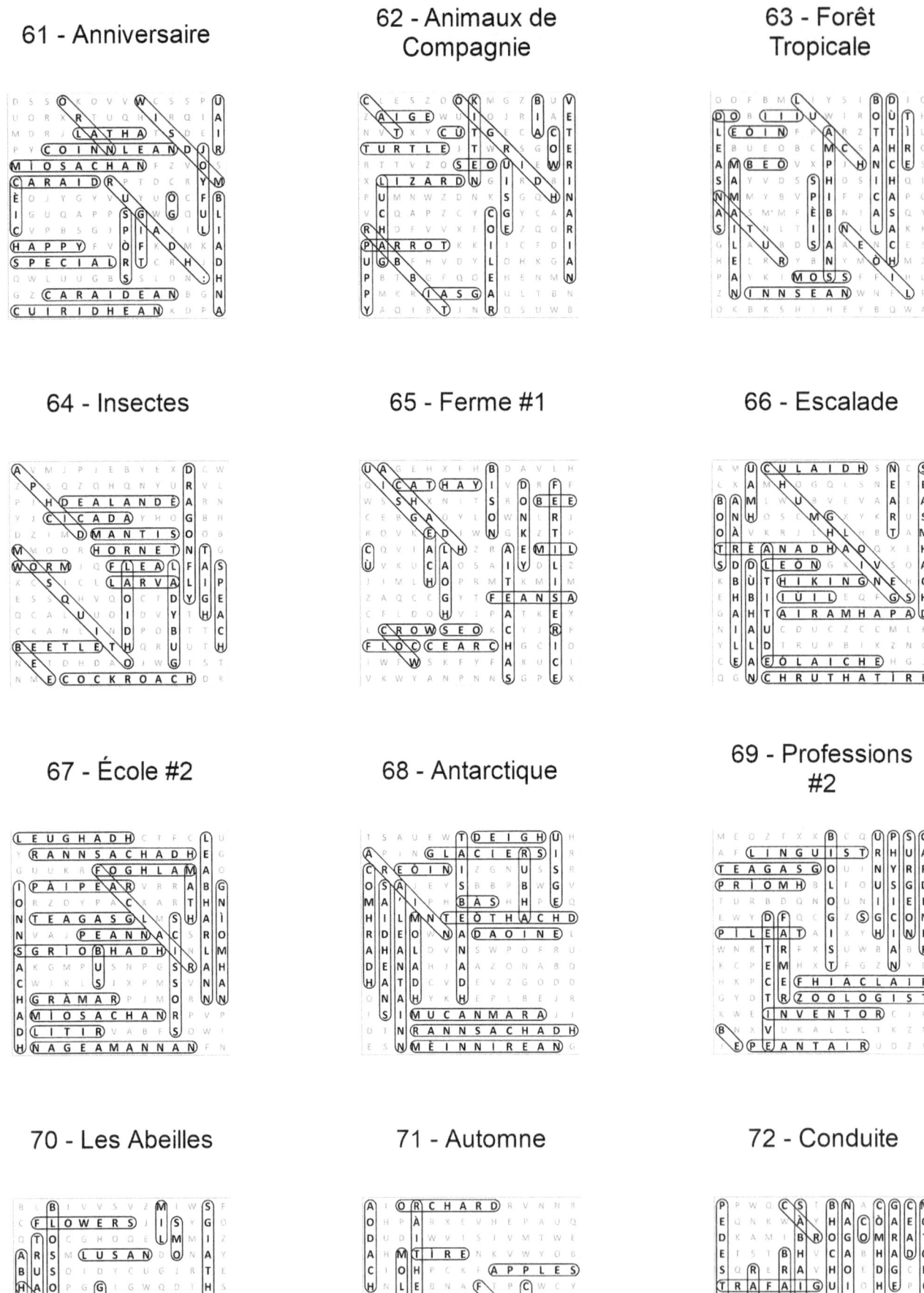

73 - Plantes

74 - Ferme #2

75 - École #1

76 - Vacances #2

77 - Outils

78 - Temps

79 - Maison

80 - Légumes

81 - Plage

82 - Vacances #1

83 - Famille

84 - Oiseaux

85 - Disciplines Scientifiques

86 - Géographie

87 - Danse

88 - Bâtiments

89 - Pêche

90 - Activités et Loisirs

91 - Livres

92 - Pays #2

93 - Fournitures d'Art

94 - Jouets

95 - Eau

96 - Paysages

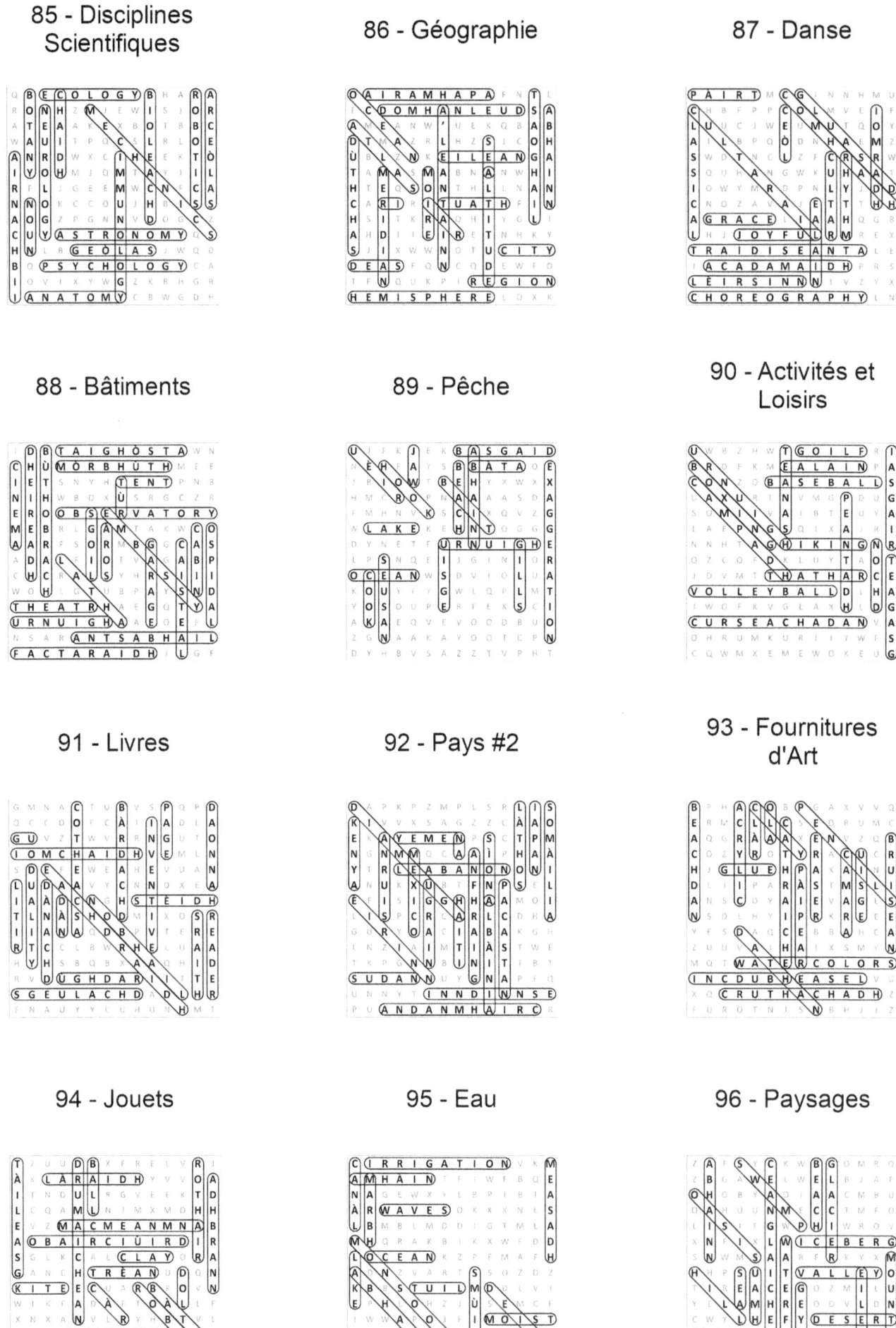

97 - Nombres

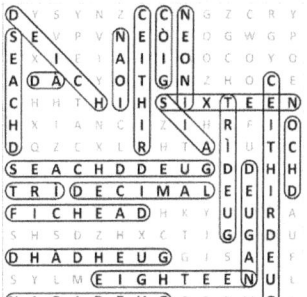

98 - Nature

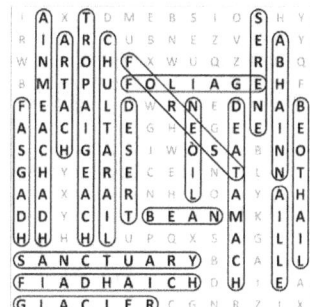

99 - Bateaux

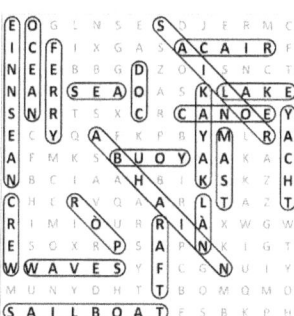

100 - Mesures

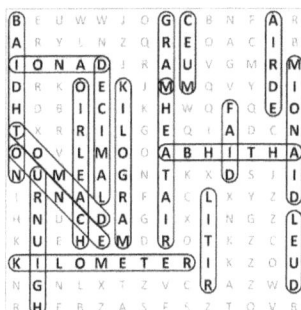

Dictionnaire

Activités
Gnìomhan

Activité	Cleas
Art	Ealain
Artisanat	Obair-Ciùird
Camping	Campadh
Chasse	Sealg
Compétence	Sgil
Couture	Seòrr
Danse	Dannsa
Lecture	Leughadh
Loisir	Cur-Seachadan
Magie	Magic
Peinture	Peantadh
Pêche	Iasgair
Photographie	Photography
Plaisir	Pleasure
Randonnée	Hiking
Relaxation	Laoidh
Tricot	Fighe

Activités et Loisirs
Cleasan is Cur-Seachadan

Art	Ealain
Base-Ball	Baseball
Basket-Ball	Thathar
Boxe	Boxing
Camping	Campadh
Golf	Goilf
Nager	Nochd
Passe-Temps	Cur-Seachadan
Peinture	Peantadh
Pêche	Iasgair
Randonnée	Hiking
Surf	Urnuigh
Tennis	Teanas
Volley-Ball	Volleyball
Voyage	Teagasg

Adjectifs #1
Buadhairean # 1

Absolu	Gu Math
Actif	Gnìomhach
Ambitieux	Adhartach
Aromatique	Aromatic
Attractif	Tarraingiche
Beau	Bòidheach
Exotique	Moladh
Énorme	Mòr
Fantastique	Sgoinneil
Généreux	Chuid
Honnête	Honest
Important	Cudromach
Innocent	Neo-Chiontach
Jeune	Òg
Lent	Laoidh
Lourd	Heavy
Mince	Thin
Parfait	Perfect
Profond	Deep
Utile	Feumail

Adjectifs #2
Buadhairean # 2

Authentique	Fìor
Célèbre	Ainmeil
Créatif	Cruthachail
Descriptif	Descriptive
Doué	Ga Thoirt
Dramatique	Dràma
Élégant	Elegant
Fier	Proud
Fort	Strong
Intéressant	Inntinneach
Naturel	Nàdarra
Nouveau	Ùr
Productif	A Bhith A
Puissant	Cumhachd
Pur	Eile.
Responsable	Freagrach
Sain	Slàinte
Salé	Salty
Sauvage	Fiadhaich
Somnolent	Sleepy

Animaux de Compagnie
Peataichean

Chat	Cat
Chaton	Kitten
Chèvre	Seo
Chien	Cù
Chiot	Puppy
Collier	Coilear
Eau	Uisge
Hamster	Òigridh
Lapin	Rabbit
Lézard	Lizard
Nourriture	Bia
Perroquet	Parrot
Poisson	Iasg
Queue	Aige
Souris	Luchag
Tortue	Turtle
Vache	Cow
Vétérinaire	Veterinarian

Anniversaire
Cho-Là-Breith

Amis	Caraidean
Amusement	Spòrs
Année	Bliadhna
Bougies	Coinnlean
Cadeau	Gift
Calendrier	Mìosachan
Cartes	Caraid
Chanson	Òran
Fête	Ceilteachadh
Gâteau	Cèic
Heureux	Happy
Invitations	Cuiridhean
Jeune	Òg
Jour	Latha
Joyeux	Joyful
Né	Rugadh:
Sagesse	Wisdom
Spécial	Special
Temps	Uair

Antarctique
An Antartaig

Baie	Bàs
Baleines	Mucan-Mara
Chercheur	Rannsachadh
Conservation	Comhradh
Continent	A 'leantainn
Eau	Uisge
Environnement	Àrainn
Expédition	Taisbeanadh
Géographie	Daoine
Glace	Deigh
Glaciers	Glaciers
Îles	Eileanan
Migration	Moladh
Minéraux	Mèinnirean
Oiseaux	Eòin
Péninsule	Rubha
Rocheux	Creagach
Scientifique	Saidheans
Température	Teòthachd
Topographie	Cruth-Tìre

Art
Ealain

Céramique	Ceramic
Complexe	Iom-Fhillte
Composition	Comhradh
Créer	Cruthaich
Expression	Iomradh
Honnête	Honest
Humeur	Mood
Inspiré	Brosnachadh
Original	Chiad Dreach
Peintures	Dealbhan
Personnel	Pearsanta
Poésie	Bàrdachd
Sculpture	Sculpture
Simple	Simplidh
Sujet	Urnuigh
Surréalisme	Surrealism
Symbole	Samhla
Visuel	Lèirsinn

Arts Visuels
Na H-Ealain Lèirsinne

Architecture	Ailtireachd
Argile	Clay
Artiste	Ealain
Chef-D'Œuvre	Masterpiece
Chevalet	Easel
Cire	Wax
Composition	Comhradh
Craie	Chalk
Crayon	Peann
Créativité	Cruthachadh
Film	Film
Peinture	Peantadh
Perspective	Sealladh
Photographie	Dealbh-Camara
Pochoir	Stencil
Portrait	Dealbh
Sculpture	Sculpture

Astronomie
Reul-Eòlas

Astéroïde	Asteroid
Astronaute	Prìomh
Astronome	Astronomer
Ciel	Sky
Constellation	Constellation
Cosmos	Cosmos
Éclipse	Crìonadh
Équinoxe	Equinox
Fusée	Rocaid
Galaxie	Galaxy
Lune	Moon
Météore	Meteor
Nébuleuse	Nebula
Observatoire	Observatory
Planète	Planet
Radiation	Rèididheachd
Solaire	Panalan
Supernova	Stephens
Terre	An Talamh
Univers	Urnuigh

Automne
As T-Fhoghar

Châtaignes	Chestnuts
Climat	Tìre
Équinoxe	Equinox
Festival	Fèis
Feux	Teintean
Gland	Acorn
Météo	Aimsir
Migration	Moladh
Mois	Mis
Nature	Natur
Pommes	Apples
Saisonnier	Ràitheil
Verger	Orchard
Vêtements	Aodach

Aventure
Dàn-Thuras

Activité	Cleas
Amis	Caraidean
Beauté	Àille
Chance	Cothrom
Dangereux	Cunnartach
Destination	Cheann-Uidhe
Défis	Dùbhalan
Difficulté	Dleasnas
Enthousiasme	Dealas
Excursion	Excursion
Itinéraire	Itinerary
Joie	Joy
Nature	Natur
Navigation	Naigheachd
Nouveau	Ùr
Préparation	Ullachadh
Sécurité	Sàbhailteachd

Avions
Plèanaichean

Air	Adhair
Altitude	Altitude
Atmosphère	An Àrd-Bhaile
Atterrissage	Talamh
Aventure	Dànachd
Ballon	Balloon
Carburant	Connadh
Ciel	Sky
Construction	Togail
Descente	Tuirling
Direction	S
Équipage	Crew
Gonfler	Inflate
Hauteur	Àirde
Histoire	Eachdraidh
Hydrogène	Hydrogen
Moteur	Einnsean
Passager	Passenger
Pilote	Pìleat
Turbulence	Turbulence

Ballet
Ballet

Chorégraphie	Choreography
Compétence	Sgil
Compositeur	Comhradh
Danseurs	Dannsairean
Expressif	Iomradh
Gracieux	Graceful
Intensité	On
Muscles	Muscles
Musique	Ceòl
Orchestre	Orchestra
Public	Urnuigh
Rythme	Rhythm
Style	Stoidhle
Technique	Technique

Barbecues
Barbecues

Chaud	Hot
Couteaux	Sgeinean
Déjeuner	Lòn
Dîner	An Dìnnear
Enfants	Clann
Été	As T-Samhradh
Faim	Acras
Famille	Teaghlach
Fruit	Measan
Gril	Grill
Jeux	Na Geamannan
Légumes	Ghlasraich
Musique	Ceòl
Oignons	Oran
Poivre	Piobar
Poulet	Cearc
Salades	Salads
Sauce	Sauce
Sel	Salann
Tomates	Tomatoes

Bateaux
Bàtaichean

Ancre	Acair
Bouée	Buoy
Canoë	Canoe
Corde	Ròp
Dock	Doc
Équipage	Crew
Ferry	Ferry
Fleuve	Abhainn
Kayak	Kayak
Lac	Lake
Marée	- Làn
Marin	Sailor
Mât	Mast
Mer	Sea
Moteur	Einnsean
Océan	Ocean
Radeau	Raft
Vagues	Waves
Voilier	Sailboat
Yacht	Yacht

Bâtiments
Togalaichean

Ambassade	Embassy
Appartement	Àros
Atelier	Bùth-Obrach
Cabine	Cabin
Château	Caisteal
Cinéma	Cinema
École	Sgoil
Garage	Garage
Grange	An T-Sabhail
Hôpital	Ospidal
Hôtel	Taigh-Òsta
Laboratoire	Latha
Observatoire	Observatory
Stade	Dheireadh
Supermarché	Mòr-Bhùth
Tente	Tent
Théâtre	Theatr
Tour	Tùr
Université	Urnuigh
Usine	Factaraidh

Camping
Campachadh

Animaux	Ainmeachadh
Aventure	Dànachd
Boussole	Iomradh
Cabine	Cabin
Canoë	Canoe
Carte	Air a ' Mhapa
Chapeau	Ad
Chasse	Sealg
Corde	Ròp
Équipement	Urnuigh
Feu	Teine
Forêt	Forest
Hamac	Hammock
Insecte	Dh'
Lac	Lake
Lanterne	Laoidh
Lune	Moon
Montagne	Moire
Nature	Natur
Tente	Tent

Championnat
Championship

Champion	Champion
Championnat	Championship
Entraîneur	Coidse
Équipe	Sgioba
Jeux	Na Geamannan
Juge	Laoidh
Ligue	Lìog
Médaille	Am Bonn
Motivation	Gluasad
Performance	Coileanadh
Sports	Spòrs
Stratégie	Ro-Innleachd
Tournoi	Farpais
Transpiration	Perspiration
Victoire	Buaidh

Châteaux
Caistealan

Armure	Armor
Bouclier	Sgiath
Catapulte	Clach-Bhogha
Cheval	Each
Chevalier	Knight
Dragon	Cathach
Dynastie	Dynasty
Empire	Empire
Épée	Sword
Féodal	Bha Fo
Forteresse	Daingnich
Licorne	Aon
Mur	Balla
Noble	Noble
Palais	Lùchairt
Prince	Prince
Princesse	Prionnsa
Royaume	Rìoghachd
Tour	Tùr

Chocolat
Chocolate

Amer	Bitter
Antioxydant	Antioxidant
Bonbon	Cola
Cacahuètes	Peanuts
Cacao	Cacao
Calories	Calories
Caramel	Caramel
Délicieux	Blasta
Doux	Sweet
Exotique	Moladh
Goût	Blas
Ingrédient	Ingredient
Noix de Coco	Coconut
Poudre	Jump
Qualité	Càileachd
Recette	Recipe
Saveur	Flavor
Sucre	Siùcair

Cirque
Siorcas

Acrobate	Acrobat
Animaux	Ainmeachadh
Astuce	Trick
Ballons	Balloons
Billet	Thiogaidean
Bonbon	Cola
Costume	Costume
Éléphant	Elephant
Jongleur	Juggler
Lion	Lion
Magie	Magic
Montrer	Seall
Musique	Ceòl
Parade	Spèis
Singe	Monkey
Spectateur	Amharc
Tente	Tent
Tigre	Tiger

Conduite
A ' Dràibheadh

Accident	Tubaist
Camion	Làraidh
Carburant	Connadh
Carte	Air a ' Mhapa
Danger	Bho Chunnart
Freins	Brakes
Garage	Garage
Gaz	Gas
Licence	Cead
Moteur	Co
Moto	Motorcycle
Piéton	Pedestrian
Police	Police
Route	Rathad
Sécurité	Sàbhailteachd
Trafic	Trafaig
Transport	Còmhdhail
Tunnel	Tunail
Vitesse	Na Gaoithe
Voiture	Càr

Conservation
Glèidhteachas

Climat	Tìre
Cycle	Cuairtich
Durable	Seasmhach
Eau	Uisge
Environnemental	Àrainneachd
Écosystème	Ecosystem
Éducation	Foghlam
Habitat	Àrainnean
Naturel	Nàdarra
Organique	Organic
Pesticide	Pesticide
Pollution	Truailleadh
Recycler	Recycle
Santé	Slàinte
Vert	Uaine

Corps Humain
Buidheann a ' Chinne-Dao

Bouche	Beul
Cerveau	Brain
Cheville	Ankle
Cou	Amhaich
Coude	Elbow
Cœur	Cridhe
Estomac	Stamag
Épaule	Sgìth
Genou	Knee
Langue	Tongue
Lèvres	Bilean
Main	Làmh
Mâchoire	Jaw
Menton	Chin
Nez	Aois
Oreille	Cluas
Peau	Skin
Sang	Dubh
Tête	Ceann
Visage	Aodann

Couleurs
Dathan

Azur	Speur-Ghorm
Beige	Beige
Blanc	Geal
Bleu	Gorm
Cyan	: Saidhean
Fuchsia	Fuchsia
Gris	Glas
Jaune	Buidhe
Magenta	Maidèanta Ann
Marron	Donn
Noir	Dubh
Orange	Orains
Rose	Pink
Rouge	Red
Sépia	Sepia
Vert	Uaine
Violet	Purpaidh

Cuisine
A ' Chidsin

Baguettes	Chopsticks
Bol	Bobhla
Congélateur	Freezer
Couteaux	Sgeinean
Cruche	Jug
Cuillères	Juice
Épices	Laoidhean
Éponge	Sponge
Four	Àmhainn
Fourchettes	Forks
Gril	Grill
Nourriture	Bia
Pot	Jar
Recette	Recipe
Réfrigérateur	Carbad
Serviette	Napkin
Tablier	Apron
Tasses	Copain

Danse
Dannsa

Académie	Acadamaidh
Art	Ealain
Chorégraphie	Choreography
Classique	Classical
Corps	Comhradh
Culture	Cultar
Culturel	Cultarail
Expressif	Iomradh
Grâce	Grace
Joyeux	Joyful
Mouvement	Gluasad
Musique	Ceòl
Partenaire	Pàirt
Rythme	Rhythm
Traditionnel	Traidiseanta
Visuel	Lèirsinn

Disciplines Scientifiques
Smachdan Saidheansail

Anatomie	Anatomy
Archéologie	Arc-Eòlas
Astronomie	Astronomy
Biochimie	Biochemistry
Biologie	Bioleachd
Botanique	Botany
Chimie	Noun
Écologie	Ecology
Géologie	Geòlas
Immunologie	Immunology
Linguistique	Cànanachas
Mécanique	Mechanics
Météorologie	Air Nach bi I
Minéralogie	Mineralogy
Neurologie	Neurology
Physiologie	Physiology
Psychologie	Psychology
Robotique	Robotics
Sociologie	Chaidh
Zoologie	Contributions

Eau
Uisge

Canal	Canàl
Douche	A-Mhàin
Évaporation	Measadh
Fleuve	Abhainn
Geyser	Geyser
Glace	Deigh
Humidité	Moist
Inondation	Tuil
Irrigation	Irrigation
Lac	Lake
Mousson	Monsoon
Neige	Snow
Océan	Ocean
Ouragan	Marbh
Vagues	Waves
Vapeur	Smùid

Escalade
Streap

Altitude	Altitude
Atmosphère	An Àrd-Bhaile
Blessure	Leòn
Bottes	Boots
Carte	Air a ' Mhapa
Casque	Culaidh
Défis	Dùbhalan
Expert	Eòlaiche
Étroit	Chumhaing
Force	Neart
Formation	Trèanadh
Gants	Gloves
Grotte	Uamh
Guides	Iùil
Physique	S
Randonnée	Hiking
Stabilité	Seasmhachd
Terrain	Chrutha-Tìre

Échecs
Tàileasg

Blanc	Geal
Champion	Champion
Défis	Dùbhalan
Diagonal	Diagonal
Jeu	Geama
Joueur	Player
Noir	Dubh
Passif	Passive
Reine	A ' Bhanrigh
Règles	Riaghailtean
Roi	Ring
Sacrifice	Ìobairt
Stratégie	Ro-Innleachd
Temps	Uair
Tournoi	Farpais

École #1
Sgoil # 1

Alphabet	Aibideil
Amis	Caraidean
Amusement	Spòrs
Bibliothèque	Leabharlann
Bureau	Deasg
Chaise	Cathraiche
Crayon	Peann
Des Stylos	Pens
Déjeuner	Lòn
Dossiers	Pasganan
Enseignant	Teagasg
Examens	Exams
Livres	Leabhraichean
Math	Math
Nombres	Àireamhan
Papier	Pàipear
Réponses	Freagairtean
Salle de Classe	Seòmar-Sgoile

École #2
Sgoil # 2

Activités	Gnìomhan
Apprentissage	Ionnsachadh
Bibliothèque	Leabharlann
Bus	Bus
Calendrier	Mìosachan
Ciseaux	Scissors
Crayon	Peann
Dictionnaire	Faclair
Enseignant	Teagasg
Écriture	Sgrìobhadh
Éducation	Foghlam
Grammaire	Gràmar
Jeux	Na Geamannan
Lecture	Leughadh
Littérature	Litir
Livres	Leabhraichean
Math	Math
Ordinateur	Rannsachadh
Papier	Pàipear
Science	Saidhean

Écologie
Eag-Eòlas

Climat	Tìre
Diversité	Dleasnas
Durable	Seasmhach
Faune	Ainmhidhean
Flore	Flòraidh
Global	Cruinne
Habitat	Àrainnean
Marais	Marsh
Marin	Mara
Nature	Natur
Naturel	Nàdarra
Plantes	Lusan
Ressources	Goireasan
Sécheresse	Drought
Survie	Beò
Variété	Barantas
Végétation	Laoidh

Épices
Spìosraidhean

Aigre	Sour
Amer	Bitter
Anis	Anise
Cannelle	Cinnamon
Cardamome	Cardamom
Coriandre	Coriander
Cumin	Cumin
Curry	Curry
Fenouil	Fennel
Fenugrec	Fenugreek
Gingembre	Ginger
Muscade	Nutmeg
Oignon	Onion
Paprika	Paprika
Poivre	Piobar
Réglisse	Licorice
Safran	Saffron
Saveur	Flavor
Sel	Salann
Vanille	Vanilla

Été
As T-Samhradh

Amis	Caraidean
Camping	Campadh
Étoiles	Stars
Famille	Teaghlach
Jardin	Garden
Jeux	Na Geamannan
Joie	Joy
Livres	Leabhraichean
Loisir	Cur-Seachadan
Mer	Sea
Musique	Ceòl
Nourriture	Bia
Plage	Beach
Relaxation	Laoidh
Sandales	Sandals
Vacances	Vacation
Voyage	Teagasg

Famille
Teaghlach

Ancêtre	Ancestor
Cousin	Co-Ogha
Enfance	A H-Òige,
Enfant	Clann
Femme	Bean
Fille	Nighean
Frère	Brother
Grand-Mère	Seanmhair
Grand-Père	Seanair
Mari	Duine
Maternel	Maternal
Mère	Màthair
Neveu	Nephew
Nièce	Cuimhne
Oncle	Uair
Paternel	Paternal
Petit-Fils	An T-Ogha,
Père	Athair
Soeur	Piuthar
Tante	Aunt

Ferme #1
Tuathanas # 1

Abeille	Bee
Agriculture	Àiteachas
Âne	Donkey
Bison	Bison
Champ	Achadh
Chat	Cat
Cheval	Each
Chèvre	Seo
Chien	Cù
Clôture	Feansa
Corbeau	Crow
Eau	Uisge
Engrais	Fertiliser
Foin	Hay
Miel	Mil
Poulet	Cearc
Riz	Rice
Troupeau	Floc
Vache	Cow
Veau	Laogh

Ferme #2
Tuathanas # 2

Agneau	Litir
Agriculteur	Farmer
Animaux	Ainmeachadh
Blé	Chruithneachd
Canard	Tunnag
Fruit	Measan
Grange	An T-Sabhail
Irrigation	Irrigation
Lait	Bainne
Lama	Llama
Légume	Glasraich
Maïs	Coirce
Moulin à Vent	Windmill
Mouton	Duilleag
Nourriture	Bia
Oies	Geòidh
Orge	Barley
Pré	Meadow
Tracteur	Tractar
Verger	Orchard

Fleurs
Flùraichean

Bouquet	Bouquet
Gardénia	Gardenia
Hibiscus	Hibiscus
Jasmin	Jasmine
Lavande	Laoidh
Lilas	Lilac
Lys	Lily
Magnolia	Magnolia
Marguerite	Daisy
Orchidée	Orchid
Pavot	Poppy
Pétale	Petal
Pissenlit	Dandelion
Pivoine	Peony
Plumeria	Plumeria
Tournesol	Sunflower
Trèfle	Seamraig
Tulipe	Tulip

Forêt Tropicale
Coille-Uisge

Amphibiens	Amphibians
Botanique	Botanical
Climat	Tìre
Diversité	Dleasnas
Indigène	Dùthchasach
Insectes	Innsean
Mammifères	Mamailean
Mousse	Moss
Nature	Natur
Nuage	Neòil
Oiseaux	Eòin
Précieux	Luach
Refuge	Do
Respect	Spèis
Restauration	Iii
Survie	Beò

Formes
Cumaidhean

Arc	Arc
Bords	Iomallan
Carré	Ceann
Cercle	Cearcall
Coin	Oisean
Courbe	Curve
Cône	Cone
Côté	Taobh
Cube	Cube
Cylindre	Siolandair
Ellipse	Ellipse
Hyperbole	Hyperbola
Ligne	Line
Ovale	Oval
Polygone	Polygon
Prisme	Prism
Pyramide	Pyramid
Triangle	Triantan

Fournitures d'Art
Ealain Bathair

Acrylique	Acrylic
Aquarelles	Watercolors
Argile	Clay
Brosses	Bruisean
Caméra	Camara
Chaise	Cathraiche
Chevalet	Easel
Colle	Glue
Couleurs	Dathan
Crayons	Pencils
Créativité	Cruthachadh
Eau	Uisge
Encre	Inc Dubh
Gomme	Eraser
Huile	Ola
Idées	Beachdan
Papier	Pàipear
Table	Clàr

Fruit
Measan

Abricot	Apricot
Ananas	Pineapple
Avocat	Avocado
Baie	Berry
Banane	Banana
Cerise	Cherry
Citron	Lemon
Figue	Fig
Framboise	Raspberry
Goyave	Guava
Kiwi	Kiwi
Mangue	Mango
Melon	Melon
Nectarine	Nectarine
Orange	Orains
Papaye	Papaya
Pêche	Peach
Poire	Peuran
Pomme	Apple
Raisin	Grape

Gentillesse
Coibhneas

Aimant	Laoidh
Amical	Friendly
Attentif	Attentive
Authentique	Fhìor
Compatissant	Iomradh
Compréhension	Tuigse
Fiable	Earbsach
Généreux	Chuid
Heureux	Happy
Honnête	Honest
Hospitalier	Ospidal
Patient	Euslainteach
Respectueux	Modhail
Réceptif	Faighinn
Tolérant	Ceadachail
Utile	Feumail

Géographie
Cruinn-Eòlas

Altitude	Altitude
Atlas	Atlas
Carte	Air a ' Mhapa
Continent	A 'leantainn
Fleuve	Abhainn
Hémisphère	Hemisphere
Île	Eilean
Latitude	Domhan-Leud
Mer	Sea
Méridien	Meridian
Monde	T-Saoghail
Montagne	Moire
Nord	Tuath
Océan	Ocean
Ouest	Iar
Pays	Dùthchas
Région	Region
Sud	Deas
Territoire	Ri
Ville	City

Géologie
Geòlas

Acide	Acid
Calcium	Calcium
Caverne	Cavern
Continent	A 'leantainn
Corail	Coral
Couche	Laoidh
Cristaux	Crystals
Fondu	Molten
Fossile	Fossil
Geyser	Geyser
Lave	Lava
Minéraux	Mèinnirean
Pierre	Caraid
Plateau	Àrd-Chlàr A'
Quartz	Quartz
Sel	Salann
Stalactite	Stalactite
Stalagmites	Stalagmites
Volcan	Volcano
Zone	Zone

Herboristerie
Luibh-Eòlas

Aromatique	Aromatic
Basilic	Basil
Bénéfique	Fear-Ciuil
Culinaire	Culinary
Estragon	Tarragon
Fenouil	Fennel
Fleur	Flùr
Ingrédient	Ingredient
Jardin	Garden
Lavande	Laoidh
Marjolaine	Meacan-Dubh
Menthe	Mint
Origan	Oregano
Persil	Parsley
Qualité	Càileachd
Romarin	Rosemary
Safran	Saffron
Saveur	Flavor
Thym	Thyme
Vert	Uaine

Insectes
Meanbh-Bhiastagan

Abeille	Bee
Cafard	Cockroach
Cigale	Cicada
Coccinelle	Ladybug
Criquet	Laoidh
Frelon	Hornet
Guêpe	Speach
Larve	Larva
Libellule	Dragonfly
Mante	Mantis
Moustique	Mosquito
Papillon	Dealan-Dè
Puce	Flea
Puceron	Aphid
Scarabée	Beetle
Termite	Taigh
Ver	Worm

Instruments de Musique
Ionnsramaidean Ciùil

Banjo	Banjo
Basson	Bassoon
Clarinette	Clarinet
Flûte	Flùr
Gong	Gong
Guitare	Giotàr
Harpe	Clàrsach
Hautbois	Oboe
Mandoline	Mandolin
Marimba	Marimba
Percussion	Faraim
Piano	Piano
Saxophone	Sacsafon
Tambour	Drum
Tambourin	Tambairin
Trombone	Trompan
Trompette	Trumpet
Violon	Violin
Violoncelle	Cello

Jardin
Garden

Arbre	Tree
Banc	Fear
Buisson	Bush
Clôture	Feansa
Étang	Lochan
Fleur	Flùr
Garage	Garage
Hamac	Hammock
Herbe	Gras
Jardin	Garden
Mauvaises Herbes	Hawk'
Pelle	Sluasaid
Pelouse	Glasach
Râteau	Rake
Sol	Ùir
Terrasse	Terrace
Trampoline	Trampoline
Tuyau	Oran
Verger	Orchard
Vigne	Vine

Jouets
Dèideagan

Argile	Clay
Artisanat	Obair-Ciùird
Avion	Adhbrann
Balle	Ball
Bateau	Bàta
Camion	Làraidh
Cerf-Volant	Kite
Échecs	Tàileasg
Imagination	Mac-Meanmna
Jeux	Na Geamannan
Livres	Leabhraichean
Poupée	Dol
Puzzle	Tòimhseachan
Robot	Robot
Tambours	Drumaichean
Train	Trèan
Vélo	Rothair
Voiture	Càr

Jours et Mois
Làithean Agus Mìosan

Août	An Lùnastal
Avril	A 'Ghiblean
Calendrier	Mìosachan
Décembre	An Dùbhlachd
Dimanche	Didòmhnaich
Février	An Gearran
Jeudi	Diardaoin
Juillet	An T-Iuchar
Juin	An T-Ògmhios
Lundi	Diluain
Mardi	Dimàirt
Mars	Am Màrt
Mercredi	Diciadain
Mois	Mìos
Novembre	An T-Samhain
Octobre	An Dàmhair
Samedi	Disathairne
Semaine	Seachdain
Septembre	An T-Sultain
Vendredi	Dihaoine

Les Abeilles
Seilleanan

Ailes	Sgiathan		
Bénéfique	Fear-Ciuil		
Cire	Wax		
Diversité	Dleasnas		
Essaim	Swarm		
Écosystème	Ecosystem		
Fleur	Blossom		
Fleurs	Flowers		
Fruit	Measan		
Fumée	Smo		
Habitat	Àrainnean		
Insecte	Dh'		
Jardin	Garden		
Miel	Mil		
Nourriture	Bia		
Plantes	Lusan		
Pollen	Truailleadh		
Reine	A ' Bhanrigh		
Ruche	Hive		
Soleil	Dido		

Légumes
Ghlasraich

Algue	Feamainn
Artichaut	Artichoke
Aubergine	Eggplant
Brocoli	Broccoli
Carotte	Curran
Céleri	Celery
Champignon	Mushroom
Citrouille	Pumpkin
Concombre	Cucumber
Échalote	Shallot
Épinard	Sliasaid
Gingembre	Ginger
Navet	Turnip
Oignon	Onion
Olive	Olive
Persil	Parsley
Pois	Pea
Radis	Radish
Salade	Buileann
Tomate	Tomato

Littérature
Litreachas

Analogie	Analogy
Analyse	Mion-Sgrùdadh
Anecdote	Anecdote
Auteur	Ùghdar
Comparaison	Coimeas
Conclusion	Co-Dhùnadh
Description	Tuireadh
Dialogue	Dialogue
Fiction	Fiction
Métaphore	Metaphor
Narrateur	Stèidh
Opinion	Beachd
Poème	Dàn
Poétique	Poetic
Rime	Rhyme
Roman	Nobhail
Rythme	Rhythm
Style	Stoidhle
Thème	Thema
Tragédie	Traidseadaidh

Livres
Leabhraichean

Auteur	Ùghdar
Aventure	Dànachd
Collection	Cruinneachadh
Contexte	Co-Theacsa
Dualité	Duality
Épique	Gu
Histoire	Sgeulachd
Historique	Eachdraidh
Humoristique	Daonna
Inventif	Inventive
Lecteur	Reader
Littéraire	Litir
Narrateur	Stèidh
Page	Page
Pertinent	Iomchaidh
Poème	Dàn
Poésie	Bàrdachd
Roman	Nobhail
Série	Sraith
Tragique	Traighideach

Maison
House

Balai	Broom
Bibliothèque	Leabharlann
Chambre	Seòmar
Cheminée	Teallach
Clés	Iuchraichean
Clôture	Feansa
Cuisine	A ' Chidsin
Douche	A-Mhàin
Fenêtre	Urnuigh
Garage	Garage
Grenier	Attic
Jardin	Garden
Lampe	Lampa
Miroir	Moladh
Mur	Balla
Plafond	Ceilte
Porte	Doras
Rideaux	Curtains
Tapis	Brat
Toit	Mullach

Mammifères
Mamailean

Baleine	- Mhara
Chat	Cat
Cheval	Each
Chien	Cù
Coyote	Coyote
Dauphin	Dolphin
Éléphant	Elephant
Girafe	Sioraf
Gorille	Gorilla
Kangourou	Kangaroo
Lapin	Rabbit
Lion	Lion
Loup	Wolf
Mouton	Duilleag
Ours	Bear
Renard	Fox
Singe	Monkey
Taureau	Bull
Tigre	Tiger
Zèbre	Zebra

Mathématiques
Math

Angles	Angles
Arithmétique	Àireamhachd
Carré	Ceann
Circonférence	Circumference
Décimal	Decimal
Diamètre	Trast-Thomhas
Exposant	Easponant
Équation	Urnuigh
Fraction	Fraction
Géométrie	Geomatras
Nombres	Àireamhan
Parallèle	Parallel
Parallélogramme	Parallelogram
Périmètre	Perimeter
Polygone	Polygon
Symétrie	Symmetry
Triangle	Triantan

Mesures
Tomhais

Centimètre	Ionad
Degré	Ceum
Décimal	Decimal
Gramme	Gram
Hauteur	Àirde
Kilogramme	Kilogram
Kilomètre	Kilometer
Largeur	Leud
Litre	Litir
Longueur	Faid
Masse	Tomad
Mètre	Mheatair
Minute	Mionaid
Octet	Baidht
Once	Ounce
Poids	Urnuigh
Pouce	Òirleach
Profondeur	A Bhith A
Tonne	Ton

Meubles
Àirneis

Banc	Fear
Bibliothèque	Rùm
Bureau	Deasg
Canapé	Couch
Chaise	Cathraiche
Commode	Dresser
Coussins	Cushions
Étagères	Sgeilpichean
Futon	Futon
Hamac	Hammock
Lampe	Lampa
Lit	Leabaidh
Matelas	Mattress
Miroir	Moladh
Oreiller	Pillow
Rideaux	Curtains
Tapis	Brat

Méditation
Meditation

Acceptation	Achdan
Attention	Aire
Calme	Ciùin
Clarté	Soilleireachd
Compassion	Iomradh
Enseignements	Teagasg
Esprit	Mind
Émotions	Emotions
Éveillé	Awake
Gentillesse	Kindness
Gratitude	Chùis
Mouvement	Gluasad
Musique	Ceòl
Nature	Natur
Paix	Peace
Pensées	Thoughts
Perspective	Sealladh
Respiration	Breathadh
Silence	Sàmhchair

Météo
Aimsir

Arc-En-Ciel	Bogha-Frois
Atmosphère	An Àrd-Bhaile
Calme	Ciùin
Ciel	Sky
Climat	Tìre
Éclair	Laoidh
Glace	Deigh
Humide	Mild
Inondation	Tuil
Mousson	Monsoon
Nuage	Cloud
Nuageux	Geàrr
Ouragan	Marbh
Polaire	Polar
Sécheresse	Drought
Température	Teòthachd
Tempête	Storm
Tornade	Iomghaoth
Tropical	Tropaigeach
Vent	Urnuigh

Mythologie
Miotas-Eòlas

Archétype	Archetype
Catastrophe	Urnuigh
Ciel	Neamh
Comportement	Giùlan
Créature	Cruthachadh
Croyances	Beachdan
Culture	Cultar
Force	Neart
Guerrier	Gaisgeach
Héros	Hero
Immortalité	Immortality
Jalousie	Jealousy
Légende	Laoidh
Magique	Draoidheach
Monstre	Uile-Bhèist
Mortel	Mortal
Vengeance	Revenge

Nature
Nàdar

Abeilles	Bean
Abri	Fasgadh
Animaux	Ainmeachadh
Arctique	Artach
Beauté	Àille
Désert	Desert
Dynamique	Beothail
Feuillage	Foliage
Fleuve	Abhainn
Forêt	Forest
Glacier	Glacier
Nuage	Neòil
Paisible	Chultarail
Sanctuaire	Sanctuary
Sauvage	Fiadhaich
Serein	Serene
Tropical	Tropaigeach
Vital	Deatamach

Nombres
Àireamhan

Cinq	Còig
Deux	Dà
Décimal	Decimal
Dix	Deich
Dix-Huit	Eighteen
Dix-Neuf	Naoi-Deug
Dix-Sept	Seachd-Deug
Douze	Dhà-Dheug
Huit	Ochd
Neuf	Naoi
Quatorze	Ceithir-Deug
Quatre	Ceithir
Quinze	Deug An
Seize	Sixteen
Sept	Seachd
Six	Sia
Treize	Trì-Deug
Trois	Trì
Vingt	Fichead
Zéro	Neoni

Nourriture #1
Biadh # 1

Abricot	Apricot
Basilic	Basil
Café	Cofaidh
Cannelle	Cinnamon
Carotte	Curran
Citron	Lemon
Épinard	Sliasaid
Fraise	Strawberry
Jus	Juice
Lait	Bainne
Navet	Turnip
Oignon	Onion
Orge	Barley
Poire	Peuran
Salade	Buileann
Sel	Salann
Soupe	Sùil
Sucre	Siùcair
Thon	Tuna
Viande	Meadh

Nourriture #2
Biadh # 2

Amande	Almond
Aubergine	Eggplant
Banane	Banana
Blé	Chruithneachd
Brocoli	Broccoli
Cerise	Cherry
Céleri	Celery
Champignon	Mushroom
Chocolat	Chocolate
Jambon	Ham
Kiwi	Kiwi
Mangue	Mango
Oeuf	Ugh
Pain	Aran
Poisson	Iasg
Pomme	Apple
Poulet	Cearc
Raisin	Grape
Riz	Rice
Tomate	Tomato

Nutrition
Beathachadh

Amer	Bitter
Appétit	Appetite
Calories	Calories
Choix	Roghainn
Diète	Daithead
Digestion	Digestion
Épices	Laoidhean
Fermentation	Fermentation
Glucides	Carbohydrates
Liquides	Liquids
Nutritif	Nutrient
Poids	Urnuigh
Portion	Cuibhreann
Protéines	Proteins
Qualité	Càileachd
Santé	Slàinte
Sauce	Sauce
Saveur	Flavor
Toxine	Toxin
Vitamine	Vitamin

Océan
Ocean

Algue	Feamainn
Anguille	Easgann
Baleine	- Mhara
Bateau	Bàta
Corail	Coral
Crabe	Crab
Crevette	Seanmhair
Dauphin	Dolphin
Éponge	Sponge
Huître	Oyster
Méduse	Jellyfish
Poisson	Iasg
Poulpe	Octopus
Requin	Shark
Récif	Jersey
Sel	Salann
Tempête	Storm
Thon	Tuna
Tortue	Turtle
Vagues	Waves

Oiseaux
Eòin

Aigle	Eagle
Autruche	Ostrich
Canard	Tunnag
Canari	Canary
Cigogne	Stork
Colombe	Dove
Corbeau	Crow
Coucou	Chuthag
Cygne	Eala
Flamant	Flamingo
Moineau	Emma
Mouette	Gull
Oeuf	Ugh
Oie	Goose
Paon	Peacog
Perroquet	Parrot
Pélican	Pelican
Pigeon	Pigeon
Poulet	Cearc
Toucan	Toucan

Outils
Innealan

Agrafeuse	Stapler
Câble	Càbal
Ciseaux	Scissors
Colle	Glue
Corde	Ròp
Couteau	Sgian
Échelle	Fhàradh
Hache	Ax
Maillet	Mallet
Marteau	Hammer
Pelle	Sluasaid
Pinces	Pliers
Roue	Cuibhle
Torche	Torch
Vis	Screw

Pays #2
Dùthchannan # 2

Albanie	Albàinia
Chine	Sìona
Danemark	An Danmhairc
Ethiopie	Na
France	An Fhraing
Haïti	Haiti
Indonésie	Innd Innse
Irlande	Èirinn
Jamaïque	Diameuga
Japon	Iapan
Kenya	Kenya
Laos	Làthos
Liban	Leabanon
Mexique	Mexico
Pakistan	Pacastan
Russie	An Ruis
Somalie	Somàilia
Soudan	Sudan
Syrie	Yemen
Ukraine	Ugrain

Paysages
Cruthan-Tìre

Cascade	Waterfall
Colline	Hill
Désert	Desert
Estuaire	Ceanglaichean
Fleuve	Abhainn
Geyser	Geyser
Glacier	Glacier
Grotte	Uamh
Iceberg	Iceberg
Île	Eilean
Lac	Lake
Marais	Swamp
Mer	Sea
Montagne	Mountain
Oasis	Oasis
Péninsule	Rubha
Plage	Beach
Toundra	Tundra
Vallée	Valley
Volcan	Volcano

Pêche
Ag Iasgach

Appât	Bait
Bateau	Bàta
Branchies	Gills
Crochet	Hook
Cuire	Cook
Eau	Uisge
Exagération	Exaggeration
Fil	Uèir
Fleuve	Abhainn
Lac	Lake
Mâchoire	Jaw
Océan	Ocean
Panier	Basgaid
Plage	Beach
Poids	Urnuigh
Saison	Seusan

Pirates
Spùinneadairean

Ancre	Acair
Aventure	Dànachd
Boussole	Iomradh
Capitaine	Capal
Carte	Air a ' Mhapa
Cicatrice	Noisia
Danger	Bho Chunnart
Drapeau	Bratach
Épée	Sword
Équipage	Crew
Grotte	Uamh
Île	Eilean
Légende	Laoidh
Mauvais	Bad
Océan	Ocean
Or	Gold
Perroquet	Parrot
Pièces	Coin
Plage	Beach
Trésor	Treasure

Plage
Tràigh

Bateau	Bàta
Bleu	Gorm
Côte	A-Mhàin
Crabe	Crab
Dock	Doc
Île	Eilean
Lagune	Lagoon
Mer	Sea
Océan	Ocean
Parapluie	Umbrella
Récif	Jersey
Sable	Sand
Sandales	Sandals
Serviette	Towel
Soleil	Dido
Vacances	Vacation
Voilier	Sailboat

Plantes
Lusan

Arbre	Tree
Baie	Berry
Bambou	Bambù
Botanique	Botany
Buisson	Bush
Cactus	Cactus
Engrais	Fertiliser
Feuillage	Foliage
Fleur	Flùr
Flore	Flòraidh
Forêt	Forest
Grandir	Fàs
Haricot	Bean
Herbe	Gras
Jardin	Garden
Lierre	Ivy
Mousse	Moss
Pétale	Petal
Racine	Root
Végétation	Laoidh

Professions #1
Professions #1

Ambassadeur	Tosgaire
Astronome	Astronomer
Avocat	Neach-Lagh
Banquier	Banker
Bijoutier	Jeweler
Cartographe	Cartographer
Chasseur	Urnuigh
Danseur	Dancer
Entraîneur	Coidse
Éditeur	Deasaiche
Géologue	Geologist
Infirmière	Nurse
Médecin	Doctor
Musicien	Neach-Ciùil
Pianiste	Neach-Piàna
Plombier	Plumber
Pompier	Firefighter
Psychologue	Psychologist
Scientifique	Scientist
Vétérinaire	Veterinarian

Professions #2
Professions #2

Agriculteur	Farmer
Astronaute	Prìomh
Biologiste	Biologist
Chercheur	Rannsachadh
Chirurgien	Surgeon
Dentiste	Fhiaclair
Détective	Detective
Enseignant	Teagasg
Éditeur	Foillsichear
Illustrateur	Neach-Deilbh
Ingénieur	S
Inventeur	Inventor
Jardinier	Gardener
Journaliste	Urnuigh
Linguiste	Linguist
Médecin	Physician
Peintre	Peantair
Philosophe	B ' E
Pilote	Pìleat
Zoologiste	Zoologist

Randonnée
Coiseachd

Animaux	Ainmeachadh
Bottes	Boots
Camping	Campadh
Carte	Air a ' Mhapa
Climat	Tìre
Eau	Uisge
Fatigué	Sgìth
Guides	Iùil
Lourd	Heavy
Météo	Aimsir
Montagne	Mountain
Nature	Natur
Orientation	Comhair
Parcs	Pàirt
Pierres	Clachan
Préparation	Ullachadh
Sauvage	Fiadhaich
Soleil	Dido
Sommet	Cruinneachadh

Remplir
Ri Lìonadh

Baril	Barrel
Bassin	Cùrsa
Boîte	Box
Bouteille	Botal
Dossier	Pasgan
Enveloppe	Envelope
Panier	Basgaid
Paquet	Cur
Plateau	Tray
Poche	Pocket
Pot	Jar
Sac	Baga
Seau	Bucaid
Tiroir	Door
Tube	Tiùb
Valise	Màileid
Vase	Bhàsa

Restaurant #1
Taigh-Bìdh # 1

Allergie	Allergy
Bol	Bobhla
Café	Cofaidh
Caissier	Airgead
Couteau	Sgian
Cuisine	A ' Chidsin
Dessert	Dessert
Épicé	Spicy
Menu	Clàr-Taice
Nourriture	Bia
Pain	Aran
Poulet	Cearc
Réservation	Moladh
Sauce	Sauce
Serveuse	Waitress
Serviette	Napkin
Viande	Meadh

Restaurant #2
Taigh-Bìdh # 2

Boisson	Deoch
Chaise	Cathraiche
Cuillère	Spoon
Déjeuner	Lòn
Délicieux	Blasta
Dîner	An Dìnnear
Eau	Uisge
Épices	Laoidhean
Fourchette	Gobhal
Fruit	Measan
Gâteau	Cèic
Glace	Deigh
Légumes	Ghlasraich
Nouilles	Noodles
Oeuf	Uighean
Poisson	Iasg
Salade	Buileann
Sel	Salann
Serveur	Waiter
Soupe	Sùil

Salle de Bains
Taigh-Beag

Bain	Bath
Bulles	Bataraidhean
Ciseaux	Scissors
Douche	A-Mhàin
Eau	Uisge
Éponge	Sponge
Lotion	Laoidh
Miroir	Moladh
Parfum	Perfume
Robinet	Faucet
Savon	Siabann
Serviette	Towel
Shampooing	Shampoo
Tapis	Brat
Toilette	Taigh Beag
Vapeur	Smùid

Science
Saidheans

Atome	Atom
Chimique	Chemical
Climat	Tìre
Données	Dàta
Expérience	E
Évolution	Evolution
Fait	S
Fossile	Fossil
Gravité	Gravity
Hypothèse	Hypothesis
Laboratoire	Latha
Méthode	Modh
Minéraux	Mèinnirean
Molécules	Molecules
Nature	Natur
Observation	Sealladh
Particules	Com-Pàirtean
Physique	Fisic
Plantes	Lusan
Scientifique	Scientist

Science-Fiction
Ficsean-Saidheans

Atomique	Atomic
Cinéma	Cinema
Dystopie	Dystopia
Explosion	Spreadhadh
Extrême	Àirde
Fantastique	Sgoinneil
Feu	Teine
Futuriste	Futuristic
Galaxie	Galaxy
Illusion	Illusion
Imaginaire	Imaginary
Livres	Leabhraichean
Monde	T-Saoghail
Mystérieux	Mysterious
Oracle	Oracle
Planète	Planet
Robots	Robots
Technologie	Teicneòlas
Utopie	Utopia

Sports
Spòrs

Arbitre	Rèitear
Athlète	Athlete
Base-Ball	Baseball
Basket-Ball	Thathar
Championnat	Championship
Entraîneur	Coidse
Équipe	Sgioba
Gagnant	Taghaidh
Golf	Goilf
Gymnase	Gymnasium
Gymnastique	Gymnastics
Hockey	Hocaidh
Jeu	Geama
Joueur	Player
Mouvement	Gluasad
Stade	Dheireadh
Tennis	Teanas
Vélo	Rothair

Surf
Surfadh

Français	Gàidhlig
Amusement	Spòrs
Athlète	Athlete
Champion	Champion
Débutant	Tòiseachaidh
Estomac	Stamag
Extrême	Àirde
Force	Neart
Foules	Crowds
Météo	Aimsir
Mousse	Foam
Océan	Ocean
Plage	Beach
Populaire	Seo
Récif	Jersey
Style	Stoidhle
Vague	Wave
Vitesse	Na Gaoithe

Technologie
Teicneòlas

Français	Gàidhlig
Blog	Blog
Caméra	Camara
Curseur	Cursor
Données	Dàta
Écran	Sgrìn
Fichier	Faidhle
Internet	Eadar-Lìon
Logiciel	Bathar-Bog
Message	Fear-Tathaich
Navigateur	Bhrabhsair
Numérique	Didseatach
Octets	Bytes
Ordinateur	Rannsachadh
Police	Cruth-Clò
Sécurité	Dèanamh
Statistiques	Statistics
Virtuel	Mas-Fhìor
Virus	Virus

Temps
Uair

Français	Gàidhlig
Année	Bliadhna
Annuel	Bliadhnail
Après	A-Mhàin
Avant	Mus
Bientôt	Urnaigh
Calendrier	Mìosachan
Décennie	Deichead
Futur	Àm ri Teachd
Heure	Uair
Hier	An-Dè
Horloge	Cloc
Jour	Latha
Maintenant	A-Nis
Matin	Madainn
Midi	Chan Eil
Minute	Mionaid
Mois	Mìos
Nuit	Oidhche
Semaine	Seachdain
Siècle	Linn

Types de Cheveux
Seòrsan Fuilt

Français	Gàidhlig
Blanc	Geal
Blond	Blar
Boucles	Curls
Brillant	Shiny
Chauve	Bald
Coloré	Dathte
Court	Goirid
Doux	Soft
Épais	Tiugh
Frisé	Curly
Gris	Glas
Lisse	Mìn
Long	Fad
Marron	Donn
Mince	Thin
Noir	Dubh
Ondulé	Mfu
Sain	Slàinte
Tresses	Braid
Tressé	Pleatach

Vacances #1
Làithean-Saora # 1

Français	Gàidhlig
Avion	Adhbrann
Billet	Thiogaidean
Devise	Airgeadra
Départ	Roinn
Douane	Customan
Expédition	Taisbeanadh
Itinéraire	Itinerary
Lac	Lake
Parapluie	Umbrella
Relaxation	Laoidh
Sac à Dos	Backpack
Touriste	Turas
Tram	Trama
Valise	Màileid
Voiture	Càr

Vacances #2
Làithean-Saora # 2

Français	Gàidhlig
Aéroport	Airport
Camping	Campadh
Carte	Air a ' Mhapa
Destination	Cheann-Uidhe
Étranger	Cèin
Hôtel	Taigh-Òsta
Île	Eilean
Loisir	Cur-Seachadan
Mer	Sea
Passeport	Passport
Photos	Dealbhan
Plage	Beach
Réservations	Molaidhean
Taxi	Tacsaidh
Tente	Tent
Train	Trèan
Transport	Còmhdhail
Vacances	Laoidh
Visa	Visa
Voyage	Turas

Vertus #1
Buadhan # 1

Bon	Math
Charmant	Geasach
Curieux	Gu Math
Décisif	Decisive
Drôle	Funny
Efficace	Èifeachd
Fiable	Earbsach
Généreux	Chuid
Indépendant	Urnuigh
Intelligent	Innealan
Modeste	Modest
Passionné	Seo
Patient	Euslainteach
Pratique	Practaigeach
Propre	Clean
Sage	Wise
Utile	Feumail

Véhicules
Carbadan

Avion	Adhbrann
Bateau	Bàta
Bus	Bus
Camion	Làraidh
Caravane	Caravan
Ferry	Ferry
Fusée	Rocaid
Hélicoptère	Heileacoptair
Métro	Subway
Moteur	Co
Navette	Shuttle
Pneus	Tires
Radeau	Raft
Scooter	Scooter
Sous-Marin	Submarine
Taxi	Tacsaidh
Tracteur	Tractar
Train	Trèan
Vélo	Rothair
Voiture	Càr

Vêtements
Aodach

Bracelet	Bracelet
Ceinture	Na H-Alba
Chapeau	Ad
Chaussure	Shoe
Chemise	Lèine
Chemisier	Blouse
Collier	Necklace
Foulard	Scarf
Gants	Gloves
Jeans	Jeans
Jupe	Sìos
Manteau	Mapa
Mode	Fasain
Pantalon	Pants
Pull	Sweater
Pyjama	Pajamas
Robe	Doctor
Sandales	Sandals
Tablier	Apron
Veste	Seacaid

Ville
Am Baile

Aéroport	Airport
Banque	Ban
Bibliothèque	Leabharlann
Boulangerie	Taigh-Fuine
Cinéma	Cinema
Clinique	Clionaig Ùr
École	Sgoil
Fleuriste	Florist
Galerie	Gàrradh
Hôtel	Taigh-Òsta
Librairie	Bookstore
Magasin	Stòr
Marché	Market
Pharmacie	Pharmacy
Stade	Dheireadh
Supermarché	Mòr-Bhùth
Théâtre	Theatr
Université	Urnuigh
Zoo	Sù

Félicitations

Vous avez réussi !

Nous espérons que vous avez apprécié ce livre autant que nous avons pris plaisir à le concevoir. Nous faisons de notre mieux pour créer des livres de la meilleure qualité possible.
Cette édition est conçue pour permettre un apprentissage intelligent et de qualité en se divertissant !

Vous avez aimé ce livre ?

Une Simple Demande

Nos livres existent grâce aux avis que vous publiez. Pourriez-vous nous aider en laissant un avis maintenant ?

Voici un lien rapide qui vous mènera à votre page d'évaluation de vos commandes :

BestBooksActivity.com/Avis50

CHALLENGE FINAL !

Défi n°1

Êtes-vous prêt pour votre jeu bonus ? Nous les utilisons tout le temps mais ils ne sont pas si faciles à trouver. Voici les **Synonymes** !

Notez 5 mots que vous avez trouvés dans les puzzles notés ci-dessous (n°21, n°36, n°76) et essayez de trouver 2 synonymes pour chaque mot.

Notez 5 Mots du **Puzzle 21**

Mots	Synonyme 1	Synonyme 2

Notez 5 Mots du **Puzzle 36**

Mots	Synonyme 1	Synonyme 2

Notez 5 Mots du **Puzzle 76**

Mots	Synonyme 1	Synonyme 2

Défi n°2

Maintenant que vous vous êtes échauffé, notez 5 mots que vous avez découverts dans les Puzzles n° 9, n° 17, n° 25 et essayez de trouver 2 antonymes pour chaque mot. Combien pouvez-vous en trouver en 20 minutes ?

Notez 5 Mots du **Puzzle 9**

Mots	Antonyme 1	Antonyme 2

Notez 5 Mots du **Puzzle 17**

Mots	Antonyme 1	Antonyme 2

Notez 5 Mots du **Puzzle 25**

Mots	Antonyme 1	Antonyme 2

Défi n°3

Formidable ! Ce défi final  n'est rien pour vous.

Prêt pour le dernier défi ? Choisissez 10 mots que vous avez découverts parmi les différents puzzles et notez-les ci-dessous.

1.	6.
2.	7.
3.	8.
4.	9.
5.	10.

Maintenant, composez un texte en pensant à une personne, un animal ou un lieu que vous aimez !

Astuce: Vous pouvez utiliser la dernière page de ce livre comme brouillon !

Votre Composition :

CARNET DE NOTES :

À TRÈS BIENTÔT !

Toute l'équipe

DECOUVREZ DES JEUX GRATUITS

GO

↓

BESTACTIVITYBOOKS.COM/FREEGAMES